Ratnakīrti's
Proof of Momentariness
by Positive Correlation

Kṣaṇabhaṅgasiddhi
Anvayātmikā

The American Institute of Buddhist Studies (AIBS), in affiliation with the Columbia University Center for Buddhist Studies and Tibet House US, has established the Treasury of the Buddhist Sciences series to provide authoritative English translations, studies, and editions of the texts of the Tibetan Tengyur (*bstan 'gyur*) and its associated literature. The Tibetan Tengyur is a vast collection of over 3,600 classical Indian Buddhist scientific treatises (*śāstra*) written in Sanskrit by over 700 authors from the first millennium CE, now preserved mainly in systematic 7th–12th century Tibetan translation. Its topics span all of India's "outer" arts and sciences, including linguistics, medicine, astronomy, socio-political theory, ethics, art, and so on, as well as all of her "inner" arts and sciences such as philosophy, psychology ("mind science"), meditation, and yoga.

THE DALAI LAMA

Letter of Support

The foremost scholars of the holy land of India were based for many centuries at Nālandā Monastic University. Their deep and vast study and practice explored the creative potential of the human mind with the aim of eliminating suffering and making life truly joyful and worthwhile. They composed numerous excellent and meaningful texts. I regularly recollect the kindness of these immaculate scholars and aspire to follow them with unflinching faith. At the present time, when there is great emphasis on scientific and technological progress, it is extremely important that those of us who follow the Buddha should rely on a sound understanding of his teaching, for which the great works of the renowned Nālandā scholars provide an indispensable basis.

In their outward conduct the great scholars of Nālandā observed ethical discipline that followed the Pāli tradition, in their internal practice they emphasized the awakening mind of *bodhichitta*, enlightened altruism, and in secret they practised tantra. The Buddhist culture that flourished in Tibet can rightly be seen to derive from the pure tradition of Nālandā, which comprises the most complete presentation of the Buddhist teachings. As for me personally, I consider myself a practitioner of the Nālandā tradition of wisdom. Masters of Nālandā such as Nāgārjuna, Āryadeva, Āryāsaṅga, Dharmakīrti, Candrakīrti, and Śāntideva wrote the scriptures that we Tibetan Buddhists study and practice. They are all my gurus. When I read their books and reflect upon their names, I feel a connection with them.

The works of these Nālandā masters are presently preserved in the collection of their writings that in Tibetan translation we call the Tengyur (*bstan 'gyur*). It took teams of Indian masters and great Tibetan translators over four centuries to accomplish the historic task of translating them into Tibetan. Most of these books were later lost in their Sanskrit originals, and relatively few were translated into Chinese. Therefore, the Tengyur is truly one of Tibet's most precious treasures, a mine of understanding that we have preserved in Tibet for the benefit of the whole world.

Keeping all this in mind I am very happy to encourage a long-term project of the American Institute of Buddhist Studies, originally established by the late Venerable Mongolian Geshe Wangyal and now at the Columbia University Center for Buddhist Studies, and Tibet House US, to translate the Tengyur into English and other modern languages, and to publish the many works in a collection called *The Treasury of the Buddhist Sciences*. When I recently visited Columbia University, I joked that it would take those currently working at the Institute at least three "reincarnations" to complete the task; it surely will require the intelligent and creative efforts of generations of translators from every tradition of Tibetan Buddhism, in the spirit of the scholars of Nālandā, although we may hope that using computers may help complete the work more quickly. As it grows, the *Treasury* series will serve as an invaluable reference library of the Buddhist Sciences and Arts. This collection of literature has been of immeasurable benefit to us Tibetans over the centuries, so we are very happy to share it with all the people of the world. As someone who has been personally inspired by the works it contains, I firmly believe that the methods for cultivating wisdom and compassion originally developed in India and described in these books preserved in Tibetan translation will be of great benefit to many scholars, philosophers, and scientists, as well as ordinary people.

I wish the American Institute of Buddhist Studies at the Columbia Center for Buddhist Studies and Tibet House US every success and pray that this ambitious and far-reaching project to create *The Treasury of the Buddhist Sciences* will be accomplished according to plan. I also request others, who may be interested, to extend whatever assistance they can, financial or otherwise, to help ensure the success of this historic project.

May 15, 2007

Ratnakīrti's Proof of Momentariness by Positive Correlation

Kṣaṇabhaṅgasiddhi
Anvayātmikā

Transliteration, Translation, and Philosophic Commentary

By
Joel Feldman and Stephen Phillips

Treasury of the Buddhist Sciences series
Tengyur Translation Initiative

Published by
The American Institute of Buddhist Studies
Columbia University's Center for Buddhist Studies
and Tibet House US

New York
2011

Tengyur Translation Initiative
Treasury of the Buddhist Sciences series
A refereed series published by:

American Institute of Buddhist Studies
Columbia University
80 Claremont Avenue, room 303
New York, NY 10027

http://www.aibs.columbia.edu

Co-published with Columbia University's Center for Buddhist Studies and Tibet House US

Distributed by Columbia University Press

Printed in the United States of America on acid-free paper.

20 19 18 17 16 15 14 13 12 11 10   5 4 3 2 1

ISBN 978-1-935011-06-4 (cloth)

Library of Congress Cataloging-in-Publication Data

Feldman, Joel, 1968-
Ratnakirti's Proof of momentariness by positive correlation : Kṣaṇabhaṅgasiddhi anvayātmikā / transliteration, translation, and philosophic commentary by Joel Feldman and Stephen Phillips.
p. cm. -- (Treasury of the Buddhist sciences series)
Includes translation from Sanskrit.
"Tengyur Translation Initiative."
Includes bibliographical references and index.
ISBN 978-1-935011-06-4 (alk. paper)
1. Ratnakīrti. Kṣaṇabhaṅgasiddhi. Anvayātmikā. 2. Yogācāra (Buddhism)--Doctrines. 3. Impermanence (Buddhism) 4. Buddhist logic. I. Phillips, Stephen, 1950- II. Ratnakīrti. Kṣaṇabhaṅgasiddhi. Anvayātmikā. English. III. Title.
BQ3300.K737F45 2011
294.3'85--dc23

2011040599

Contents

Series Editor's Preface

We are delighted to present this excellent work of philosophy from Joel Feldman and Stephen Phillips, focused on a precise and creative translation of Ratnakīrti's *Proof of Momentariness by Positive Correlations*. In translating the "Buddhist Sciences," such as are collected in the Tibetan Tengyur collection, we are ever mindful that "science," even in the imperial West, originated as "natural philosophy." It only seems nowadays to have broken free from its parent by adopting the dogma of materialism and thus shutting down metaphysics (the investigation of the nature and structure of reality) as the concern of philosophy, even though metaphysics must remain foundational to philosophy's other branches of logic, epistemology, ethics, and aesthetics. This relegation of philosophy to membership in the "humanities," the consequent launching of scientific investigation into matter and energy, and the manipulation of its results in spectacular technological applications—utterly heedless of any philosophical refinement or restraint—has changed our world dramatically. But materialist science's sophisticated analysis of the most minute elements of reality has discovered that it ultimately dissolves under analysis and so conclusively has undermined the dogma of materialism and its reductionistic triumphalism. It is no longer possible to be so sure the world has changed for the better. Rather, we are poised on the brink of planetary ecocide due to rampant over-industrialization and over-militarization caused by underdevelopment in the area of the systematic methods of cultivating individual self-restraint so highly developed long ago in the Indic sciences.

The Indian philosophical history was quite different from that of recent centuries in the West. In India, there were no dark ages during the first millennium CE, as caused in Europe where a dogmatic inquisition stifled critical inquiry under thought control in conformity to a strict set of dogmas. Vedist, Jainist, and Buddhist philosophies were all considered "inner science" (*adhyātmavidyā*), as the exploration of the individual mind and body were considered the most important realm of nature to understand and ameliorate. The education-oriented Buddhist traditions remained especially focused on the investigation of reality and its knowledge, considering those sciences aimed on the exploration and manipulation of material nature to be important, but of lesser value than the science of the mind. Years ago in a popular work, Bertrand Russell acknowledged that the Indian philosophies were unmatched in their insight into the human mind, the West in staking its claim to the exploration of physical nature, and China to society. Therefore, our long-term project of translating the treasury of Indian Buddhist inner science in a manner that is conversant with contemporary Western philosophy is potentially of global importance, as it may help to balance the West's excessive preoccupation with materialism, the backwardness of its philosophy of mind, and the clumsy chemical dependency of its reductionist psychologies.

In this effort, the philologically precise translation and philosophical recovery of Ratnakīrti's thought is a significant contribution. There is another element in the case of this particular work; although this Sanskrit text was discovered in Tibet by Dr. Rāhula Sāṅkṛtyāyana in the 1930s, where it had been preserved in the dry high altitude air for centuries, the Tibetans had apparently not gotten around to translating it into Tibetan, or if it was translated the manuscript was lost. It is not included in the existing editions of the Tengyur, though other works of Ratnakīrti are, as I will detail below. The reason may have been that the works of the great masters of Vikramaśīla that focused on refuting the Indian Vedist logicians (Naiyāyika) and other schools were not so needed in Tibet, as those schools were not live there. However, now that Tibetan Buddhism has brought the curricula and educational traditions back to India, the works are again useful. This means that our translation teams have still before them the eventual further task of translating the Sanskrit into Tibetan, so it can join Ratnakīrti's opus preserved in the Tengyur collection.

According to the American Institute of Buddhist Studies database compiled by Dr. Paul Hackett, there are twenty-four known works attributed to Ratnakīrti, some extant only in Tibetan, some extant only in Sanskrit, and some extant in both. The works extant only in Sanskrit are:

1. apohasiddhi
2. avayavinirākaraṇa
3. citrādvaitasiddhi or –prakāśa
4. īśvara(sādhana)dūṣaṇa
5. kalyāṇakāṇḍaprakaraṇa
6. kṣaṇabhaṅgasiddhi
7. pramāṇāntarbhavaprakaraṇa
8. sarvajñasiddhi
9. sthirasiddhidūṣaṇa [a refutation of Śaṃkara's *Sthirasiddhi*]

10. udayananirākaraṇa
11. vyāptinirṇaya
12. saṃtānāntaradūṣaṇa

The works extant only in Tibetan are:

13. yogacaturdevastotra-nāma / sbyor ba bzhi'i lha la bstod pa zhes bya ba (Toh. 1170)
14. śāsanasarvasvaka-sādhana-nāma / bstan pa'i nor thams cad pa zhes bya ba'i sgrub pa'i thabs (Toh. 1897)
15. prajñāpāramitā-maṇḍala-vidhi-nāma / shes rab kyi pha rol tu phyin pa'i dkyil 'khor gyi cho ga zhes bya ba (Toh. 2645)
16. vajravidāraṇī-sādhana-nāma / rdo rje rnam par 'joms pa'i sgrub thabs zhes bya ba (Toh. 2940)
17. vajravidāraṇīsnāna-vidhi-nāma / rdo rje rnam par 'joms pa'i khrus kyi cho ga zhes bya ba (Toh. 2941)
18. sarvadhāraṇī-sādhana-kramadvaya-nāma / gzungs thams cad kyi sgrub thabs rim pa gnyis pa zhes bya ba (Toh. 3135)
19. sarvadhāraṇī-maṇḍala-vidhi-nāma / gzungs thams cad kyi dkyil 'khor gyi cho ga zhes bya ba (Toh. 3136)
20. sarvasādhana-karma-nāma / sgrub thabs thams cad kyi las ka zhes bya ba (Toh. 3137)
21. kalyānakāṇḍa-nāma-prakaraṇa / dge ba'i sdong po zhes bya ba'i rab tu byed pa (Toh. 4080)
22. *aparyanta-vyavasthāna-prakāśakaraṇa-pradīpa / mtha' bral ma'i rnam gzhag gsal byed sgron me zhes bya ba (bka' gdams gsung 'bum phyogs sgrig, vol. 29)

The works extant in both are:

23. abhisamayālaṃkāravṛtti-kīrtikalā-nāma / mngon par rtogs pa'i rgyan gyi 'grel pa grags pa'i cha zhes bya ba (Toh. 3799)
24. dharma-viniścaya-nāma-prakaraṇa / chos rnam par nges pa zhes bya ba'i rab tu byed pa (Toh. 4084)

Potter asserts the existence of two other works attributed to Ratnakīrti, which he claims are extant in Tibetan, but provides no further information about them:

25. bhedapratibhāṣādūṣaṇa
26. saṃsargaparīkṣā

Ratnakīrti is well introduced by Feldman and Phillips, who describe his milieu during the early eleventh century at Vikramaśīla monastic university, where he seems to have studied under the renowned master, Jñānaśrīmitra. He also possibly had a scholarly and spiritual relationship with the great Atīśa, who was the most important catalyst of the "later diffusion" in Tibet of the Buddhist higher educations (*adhiśikṣa*), moral, mental, and scientific. Many of Ratnakīrti's works are focused on his debates with some of the great Vedist philosophers of the times, such as Vācaspati Miśra, Udayana, due to the invariant Buddhist emphasis on using rational debate to help others achieve what they consider "realistic worldview," and also perhaps since at this time, his great university was competing with these scholars and their schools for patronage from the Pāla dynasty rulers of that age. I congratulate Feldman and Phillips for making this portion of Ratnakīrti's defense of the (quantum) momentariness of things accessible to contemporary philosophers and Buddhist scholars. The description of their collaboration as involving sincere debate between themselves over the fine points of the reasoning is touching; it fits perfectly in the critical thinking tradition of Indian and Tibetan Buddhist universities. Of the three types of liberating wisdom (*prajñā*), the middle one, wisdom born of critical reflection (*cintāmāyīprajñā*), is powerfully mobilized in this work. Their book is our series' first presentation of the thought of one of the greatest philosophers of this late era of India's Buddhist period, and we are honored to publish these fine fruits of the authors' careful labors.

In regard to the production of the publication and the continuation of the series, I wish to thank as ever, Dr. Thomas Yarnall, my longtime student and now colleague, for his indispensable expert and meticulous assistance on all levels, from the scholarly insight and editorial revision, to the design expertise, to the publishing technicalities; Dr. Paul Hackett, for assisting in the editing as well as providing valued scholarly expertise; and Ms. Annie Bien for careful copy-editing and polishing.

Among financial benefactors and supporters, I particularly thank Mr. William T. Kistler, Mrs. Eileen Kistler, and Mr. Brian Kistler of the Kistler Foundation for their visionary recognition that amid the many crises and catastrophes afflicting the multitudes of suffering beings around the world, the recovery and translation needed to open the door for the modern mind to the inner or spiritual science of the Buddhist traditions remains a high priority for the awakening of humanity, perhaps essential to empower us to rise to the challenges we all face together at this critical planetary moment. I must also thank the staff at the Columbia University Press for their patience, cooperation and kind assistance in the distribution of the series.

Robert A.F. Thurman (Ari Genyen Tenzin Chotrag)

Jey Tsong Khapa Professor of Indo-Tibetan Buddhist Studies,
Columbia University;
President, American Institute of Buddhist Studies;
Director, Tibet House US.

Ganden Dekyi Ling
Woodstock, New York
April 25, 2010 CE
Tibetan Royal Year 2137, Year of the Iron Tiger

Author's Preface and Acknowledgements

Stephen Phillips and I have worked together on this translation and commentary for several years. We first read the text together, argued over the meaning, and came to a consensus on translation and English wording. I wrote the first draft of the commentary, but the version here has been many times improved by our discussions and editing. Both the translation and commentary went through several stages of revision. The finished product is thus the result of an interactive and critical process.

This work would not have been possible without assistance from many others. First of all, for their careful editorial attention to this work, we would like to thank Robert Thurman and Thomas Yarnall, as well as Annie Bien and Paul Hackett, of the American Institute of Buddhist Studies at Columbia University. We would also like to thank Morgan Stroud for helping us convert our formatting and the University of Texas Research Institute for providing funding.

I would also like to thank the following. First, Stephen Phillips, not only for agreeing to collaborate with me on this project, but also for all that he has taught me concerning Indian philosophy and Sanskrit. I am also grateful to Jay Garfield for inspiring my interest in Buddhist philosophy and for everything he has taught me about both philosophy and Buddhism. I wish to thank all my Sanskrit teachers, without whom I would not have been capable of producing any translation, but especially my first Sanskrit professor at the University of Texas at Austin, Edeltraud Harzer. I am also grateful to my colleagues in the Philosophy Department at Rider University, Carol Nicholson, Bob Good, and Richard Burgh for tolerating my obsession with the theory of momentariness and for helping me deepen my understanding of that topic and many others. I am also deeply grateful to my meditation teacher and dear friend, Drew Rose. Others who have provided support include Trixie Feldman, Darryl Hinko, Bill Arthurs, John Mealey, Todd Rose, Nessim Watson, Peach Watson, Hillary Simon, and Mike Morgan. Finally, let me thank Rachel Vallianos whose constant love and encouragement kept me going throughout the project.

Joel Feldman
Lawrenceville, New Jersey
March 22, 2011

PART ONE

INTRODUCTION

Introduction

Kṣaṇabhaṅgasiddhi means "proof of destruction in a moment." Ratnakīrti's text is thus an argument in support of the Buddhist doctrine of momentariness: everything that exists lasts for only a single moment and then ceases of its own accord. *Anvayātmikā* means "on the basis of positive correlation." Ratnakīrti argues that the momentariness of things follows from the fact that they exist. His inference rests upon a universal pervasion presumed between existence and momentariness. Such a pervasion can be established by positive correlations (*anvaya*)—examples of existent things that are also momentary—or by negative correlations (*vyatireka*)—examples of non-momentary things that are non-existent. Ratnakīrti accordingly divides his text into two parts: he formulates his argument on the basis of positive correlations in the Anvayātmikā, and on the basis of negative correlations in the Vyatirekātmikā. A translation of the Vyatirekātmikā, along with an explanation and analysis of the argument, has been published by McDermott (1969). Our present work consists of an English translation of the Anvayātmikā along with a transliterated text and a running commentary providing detailed explanation of each step in the argument.

In this introduction we present the relevant facts about the text and the principles we followed in producing this translation. We also discuss Ratnakīrti's life and work, placing it into the context of both the Buddhist tradition in which he worked and the Nyāya opponents against whose objections his defense of the Buddhist position is directed. In particular, we trace the history of the doctrine of momentariness and the development of the reasoning supporting the view in the centuries preceding Ratnakīrti. To facilitate an understanding of these often technical arguments, we also provide an explanation of the epistemological context which both Ratnakīrti and his Nyāya opponents assume, with special attention paid to the inferential pattern which forms the basis for both Ratnakīrti's argument and the various objections against which he defends it. We then briefly summarize Ratnakīrti's argument, reconstructing it against the backdrop of this inferential pattern.

1. Ratnakīrti and the University of Vikramaśīla

By the eleventh-century, Buddhism was on the decline in most of India, but in Bengal and Bihar, under the Pāla dynasty, it continued to flourish. At the great universities of Nālandā and Vikramaśīla, Buddhist philosophers, who were well-versed in the writings of their predecessors, keenly aware of the objections of their opponents, and armed with the more sophisticated logical tools that had been developed by this late period, offered their most rigorous formulations of arguments in favor Buddhist positions such as the theories of *apoha* (the "exclusion theory of meaning") and momentariness Ratnakīrti was an important contributor to this last great flowering of Buddhist philosophy under the Pālas, and it was at the University of Vikramaśīla that he wrote a series of sharp insightful texts on the major issues of Buddhist thought, including the *Kṣaṇabhaṅgasiddhi* (*KBS*).

Radhakrishna Chaudhary's detailed study, *The University of Vikramaśīla*, provides a wealth of information regarding the history and organization of the university, offering a tantalizing glimpse into Ratnakīrti's world.[1] Vikramaśīla was at the height of its glory when Ratnakīrti taught there in the eleventh century. Founded in the last decades of the eighth century by Dharmapāla, by the tenth century Vikramaśīla had become a thriving intellectual and cultural center, attracting students from all over the Asian world. Strong royal patronage allowed the university to grow from two hundred monks to about three thousand, and also to expand to an enormous physical size. Chaudary describes the university as having six gates enclosing an open space capable of accommodating eight to ten thousand persons. In the center was a large rectangular Chaitya, around which were one hundred and eight individual monasteries each with its own teacher. All of this was surrounded by a massive wall and fortified on all sides. Outside this wall there were one hundred and seven temples. The remains of the university have been uncovered by archeologists east of the village of Antichak.

Unlike Nālandā, which was organized democratically, the king served as the official chancellor of Vikramaśīla. Day-to-day administration was the responsibility of a council of six led by a head monk. The

---

[1] Chaudhary (1975), pp. 2–25.

curriculum was highly organized into different branches taught by specialists and systematically graded by difficulty. A wide variety of subjects were taught including medicine and astronomy. Philosophical subjects included grammar, metaphysics, and logic. *Abhidharma* ("metaphysics" or "philosophy") was an important part of the course of study. Vikramaśīla was also an important center of Tantric studies, and one could study occult science and magic. The university had very high standards of admission, which required intellectual disputation with the *dvārapaṇḍitas* ("admissions officers"). The teaching method was based upon a close relationship between the teacher and the student. Students were trained to engage in formal debate with proponents of other philosophical systems. The scholars of Vikramaśīla earned a reputation for high achievement in the formal debates which were regularly sponsored by kings where representatives of all views would participate. The language of instruction was Sanskrit, and the school had an excellent and well-maintained library containing Sanskrit texts on diverse topics including texts from all of the traditional philosophical systems of India. The diploma of the university, officially granted by the king, conferred to the graduate the degree of *paṇḍita* or *mahāpaṇḍita* ("learned scholar" and "very learned scholar").[2]

Over the years, Vikramaśīla produced many important Buddhist philosophers including Jetāri and Jñānaśrīmitra. The most influential figure was undoubtedly Atīśa, who headed the university at the time of Ratnakīrti. Atīśa was reportedly born in 982, studied under Jetāri as a young man, and took the vows of monkhood at the age of nineteen. He studied Buddhist metaphysics at both Vikramaśīla and Nālandā, where he was initiated into the Tantric tradition. At Vikramaśīla, he was reputed to be an innovative teacher and administrator, and the university apparently thrived under his leadership, becoming one of the most important centers of learning in Asia. Atīśa also traveled widely and became one of the most famous Buddhist scholars of his day.[3] In 1041, reportedly after repeated requests from Tibetan Buddhists, Atīśa left the university to bring his teachings to Tibet.[4] This second transmission of Buddhism

[2] Chaudhary (1975), pp. 18–53.

[3] Chaudhary (1975), pp. 40–43.

[4] Anantalal Thakur (1987), Introduction, p. 2.

makes Atīśa an important figure who greatly influenced Tibetan Buddhism as well, the catalyst of the "later diffusion." Atīśa's tomb can still be seen in Tibet.[5]

As a student at Vikramaśīla, Ratnakīrti studied under Jñānaśrīmitra, and we may gain some insight into Ratnakīrti's work by examining what we know about his teacher. Although we know little about the life of Jñānaśrīmitra, we know that in his writings he lists among the teachers in his lineage Prajñākaragupta, Dharmakīrti, Dignāga, Vasubandhu, and Asaṅga. He is thus the heir to a Yogācāra tradition based on the interpretation of Dharmakīrti's *Pramāṇavārtika* given by Prajñākara. His extant works cover a wide range of topics mostly in logic, metaphysics, and epistemology. He was well-versed in the philosophical techniques of his opponents, the Nyāya and Mīmāṃsā schools, and his work is said to avoid terminology that was not in use among those schools. Although A. Thakur describes Jñānaśrīmitra's work as more poetical than Ratnakīrti's, it is nonetheless quite rigorous and based on a detailed theory of inference common to the Buddhists and their opponents (see below). The opponent's arguments are typically reconstructed carefully and then refuted by showing that they exhibit various sorts of flaws. Jñānaśrīmitra quotes from a wide variety of sources from all the great Indian systems, but especially from the Nyāya school and in particular from Vācaspati Miśra, who is quoted at length and criticized in detail. He is subsequently attacked by Udayana, who defends Vācaspati Miśra.[6] The most important of Jñānaśrīmitra's works for our purposes is the *Kṣaṇabhaṅgādhyāya*, which is probably one of his early works.[7] In that text, Jñānaśrīmitra's main target is Vācaspati's teacher, Trilocana, whose arguments against momentariness are carefully evaluated and refuted. Later, Udayana defends Trilocana against the criticisms of Jñānaśrīmitra. Ratnakīrti's *KBS* Anvayātmikā is a concise reconstruction of the argument presented in the second chapter of that text. Jñānaśrīmitra and Ratnakīrti's arguments thus occupy an important place in the long debate between Buddhists and Naiyāyikas.

---

[5] Chaudhary (1975), pp. 43–47.

[6] Thakur (1987), Introduction, pp. 3–19.

[7] Thakur (1987), Introduction, p. 9.

We do not know much about Ratnakīrti himself, but we can surmise enough to make some sense of his work. If Jñānaśrīmitra is roughly the same age as Atīśa, and Ratnakīrti is ten to twenty years younger, then his date of birth must be around 1000. His works were then probably written in the first half of the eleventh century.[8] He is considered along with Atīśa and Jñānaśrīmitra to be one of the "pillars" of the university, and all three are mentioned prominently by the Tibetans. Ratnakīrti is clearly the most important of Jñānaśrīmitra's disciples, and he inherits both his teacher's rigorous logical methods and his facility with the views of his Nyāya opponents. Like his teacher, his works are wide-ranging, including writings on epistemology, metaphysics, and philosophy of language. Ratnakīrti himself is modest, saying that he merely collected a few gems from the works of Jñānaśrīmitra which he compares to an ocean.[9] His works do indeed offer more concise reconstructions of the arguments presented in a more elaborate style by Jñānaśrīmitra, but Ratnakīrti's contribution is nevertheless important, because in a very brief and elegant form he is able to capture the essence of these arguments. His work is also important because writing at such a late period, he is able to draw on the best arguments and objections on both sides of the momentariness debate. In the next century, the Pāla dynasty came to an end along with its patronage of the institution, and the university was ultimately destroyed by Muslim invaders in 1203.[10] Ratnakīrti's text thus represents one of the last moves by the Buddhists in the long debate over momentariness in the classical Indian tradition.

2. Previous Scholarship on Ratnakīrti

An early and important study of the Buddhist logicians is Satkari Mookerjee's *The Buddhist Philosophy of Universal Flux*.[11] First published in 1935, this work is remarkable in its breadth, covering topics from

---

[8] Thakur (1987), p. 2. For a detailed discussion of the issues surrounding the dates of Ratnakīrti and Jñānaśrīmitra, see Kajiyama (1998), pp. 6–11. See also Anantalal Thakur, *Ratnakīrtinibandhāvali* (1975), Introduction, pp. 14–16. Also see Etienne Lamotte (1988), p. 310.

[9] Thakur (1975), Introduction, pp. 2–14.

[10] Lamotte (1988), p. 359.

[11] Mookerjee (1975).

momentariness and the *apoha* "exclusion" theory of meaning to *nirvāna* and reincarnation, as well as expounding upon a variety of Buddhist authors and texts from various periods. Mookerjee relies heavily on Ratnakīrti's *Kṣaṇabhaṅgasiddhi* in his exposition of the theory of momentariness and paraphrases large sections of the Anvayātmikā. Mookerjee's exposition of the text is incredibly accurate, at times bordering on a word-for-word translation that admirably captures the meaning of the Sanskrit. However, the thrust of the argument is obscured by the organization of the book, which proceeds from one topic to another, incorporating discussions of the works of several authors on each topic.

His discussion of the Anvayātmikā occurs primarily in his exposiion of the relationship between momentariness and causality (see especially *Text and Translation* pp. 42–47). Mookerjee briefly but accurately runs through Ratnakīrti's responses to several objections concerning his attempt to prove momentariness on the basis of causal efficiency. Mookerjee does not, however, lay out the positive inference to which these objections are directed, assuming that the positive inference was sufficiently explained in his discussion of the negative form of the inference in the previous chapter. Instead, he just lays out these arguments along with the arguments of other authors such as Śāntarakṣita and Dharmakīrti on the role of causality in the theory of momentariness. Ratnakīrti's discussion of recognition, similarly, is covered in a later chapter as part of a long discussion of that issue by many different authors. Consequently, the particular details of Ratnakīrti's argument, scattered throughout the book along with the arguments of many other authors, are difficult to discern. Furthermore, Mookerjee tends to run together the views of all his authors and the sometimes subtle differences between them are consequently obscured in the effort to provide as much support as possible for the Buddhist view by picking what he regards as the best formulations among the various authors. In such a groundbreaking but general work, it is inevitable that nuances will be lost, and this is true of Mookerjee. This failing points up the need for a careful and sensitive examination of Ratnakīrti on his own terms. Finally, despite its usefulness, Mookerjee's account is saddled with outdated terminology. For instance, he renders *hetu* as "middle term," a practice that was in favor at the time, based on a hasty assimilation of the Indian inferential pattern to the patterns of Aristotelian syllogism. Mookerjee is sensitive to differences between the two systems, but such terminology tends to be misleading to those who are not already well-versed in Indian epistemology and logic.

In producing this study and translation, we frequently consulted A.C. Senape McDermott's translation of the Vyatirekātmikā portion of the text, published in 1969 under the title, *An Eleventh-Century Logic of 'Exists.'*[12] In explicating the text, McDermott applies logical notation developed by R. Routley in order to address contemporary issues regarding predication with respect to non-existent entities.[13] This notation certainly lends an air of rigor to the discussion, but it tends to force the argument, already rigorously formulated according to the standards of Indian logic, into the patterns of twentieth-century quantification theory. At times, the use of quantifiers does shed light on Ratnakīrti's argument by exposing, for instance, some ambiguity in the opponent's objections. But at other times it seems as though the notation is simply unnecessary, and sometimes it seems to obscure the exposition of the argument. A more serious problem with McDermott's notes is that it is not clear to what extent Routley's solution to the problem of attributions regarding unreal entities influences her account of Ratnakīrti's argument. By imposing Routley's notation and explicating the text in his terms, she runs the risk of mixing the task of a cross-cultural comparison of two solutions to a problem with the task of simply explicating one of those solutions. Before Ratnakīrti's solution can be compared to twentieth (or twenty-first) century solutions, it must first be understood on its own terms. If the text is first explicated with the application of Routley's notation, it becomes impossible to assess whether Ratnakīrti and Routley are really up to the same thing, and consequently we are left unsure whether the application of the notation was justified in the first place.

D. Seyfort Ruegg criticizes McDermott's account of Ratnakīrti's argument in an article published in *The Journal of Indian Philosophy* entitled "On Ratnakīrti," complaining that her approach was insufficiently grounded in the historical context of the Indian tradition.[14] For instance, McDermott regards Ratnakīrti as anticipating Ratnakaraśānti's theory of

---

[12] McDermott (1969).

[13] Routley (1966a and 1966b).

[14] Ruegg (1970), pp. 300–309.

antarvyāpti ("internal pervasion" or inclusion), while Ruegg points out that this is historically inaccurate given that Ratnakaraśānti was an elder contemporary of Ratnakīrti. The role of *antarvyāpti* is also an important issue in the interpretation of the text of the Anvayātmikā, and we have relied upon Ruegg's clear discussion of its relation to Ratnakīrti's argument. If the inferential subject is taken to be "everything that exists," then there are no available positive instances to support universal pervasion between existence and momentariness. Ratnakaraśānti resorts in situations like this to the method of *antarvyāpti*, drawing an example from within the inferential subject. Ratnakīrti instead relies on the method of limiting the inferential subject to cases under dispute. He then selects an arbitrary example (e.g., a pot) from outside those cases and establishes the momentariness of the example independently by showing that a bad consequence results if the object endures. This, Ruegg rightly points out, puts Ratnakīrti squarely in the mainstream tradition of Dharmakīrti, and not in the camp of Ratnakaraśānti.

In her response to Ruegg's article,[15] McDermott insists that she is arguing only that Ratnakīrti "deviated from the more conservative theory...in the course of evolving somewhat close" to the theory of *antarvyāpti*, because his inference is based upon a relation between prover and probandum which "functions as an implication operator whose logical force does not derive from the mere inductive compilation of examples." While we agree with McDermott that the reasoning behind Ratnakīrti's argument is conceptual and not empirical, this is true of any inference of the *svabhāvahetu* variety (see below), including Dharmakīrti's formulation of the argument in his *Hetubindu*. In our view, Ratnakīrti rejects *antarvyāpti* for the simple reason that it is a question-begging method. Instead he develops an argument structure that makes explicit the conceptual basis of the reasoning while remaining within the formal requirements of a valid inference. He does not, therefore, bring his tradition a step closer to *antarvyāpti*: to the contrary, he removes any temptation to rely on that fallacious method by making clear how the argument can proceed without it.

Another important work of Ratnakīrti relating to the theory of momentariness is the *Sthirasiddhidūṣaṇa*, which provides an extended response

---

[15] McDermott (1972).

to Nyāya arguments for endurance. A translation of this work into French was published by Katsumi Mimaki in 1976 under the somewhat misleading title *La Réfutation Bouddhique de la Permanence des Choses (Sthirasiddhidūṣaṇa) et la Preuve de la Momentanéité des Choses (Kṣaṇabhaṅgasiddhi)*.[16] Mimaki's book does not, however, contain a translation of the *Kṣaṇabhaṅgasiddhi*, although it does contain some discussion of Ratnakīrti's argument for momentariness along with a complete translation of the *Sthirasiddhidūṣaṇa*. We are indebted to Mimaki's work, which we consulted in relation to the discussion of Ratnakīrti's response to the objection that recognition would be impossible if all things were momentary. His glossary was particularly useful in helping us to translate various technical terms.

A series of papers by Rita Gupta on the Buddhist theory of momentariness were published in a collection entitled *Essays on Dependent Origination and Momentariness*.[17] This work, which contains excellent discussion of the arguments for momentariness of Dharmakīrti and Ratnakīrti among others, has been extremely helpful to us in understanding the development of the Buddhist theory of momentariness and the issues that surround it. The paper entitled "Ratnakīrti and some Naiyāyikas on Some Principal Issues Connected with Momentariness" contains revealing analysis of the relation between the arguments offered by Ratnakīrti and the objections raised by various philosophers from the Nyāya school. Although it does include a summary of the argument from positive correlations, the paper is primarily focused on the Vyatirekātmikā. There is an extended discussion of the positive form of the inference in "The Buddhist Doctrine of Momentariness and its Presuppositions," which insightfully brings out the key assumptions of the argument, but there Gupta focuses primarily on Dharmakīrti's *Hetubindu*, and while that work is crucial to understanding Ratnakīrti's reasoning, the peculiar details of Ratnakīrti's formulation of the argument are not taken up.

Also crucial to our understanding of Ratnakīrti's reasoning is Mokṣākaragupta's discussion of Ratnakīrti in his *Tarkabhāṣā*, which was translated into English by Yuichi Kajiyama in 1966 but not published

---

[16] Mimaki (1976).

[17] Gupta (1990).

until 1998 under the title *An Introduction to Buddhist Philosophy: An Annotated Translation of the Tarkabhāṣā of Mokṣākaragupta*.[18] In an introduction, Kajiyama discusses the relationship between Ratnakīrti, Jñānaśrīmitra, and Ratnakāraśānti. The *Tarkabhāṣā*, moreover, sheds much light on Ratnakīrti's argument. We are indebted especially to Mokṣākaragupta's comparison of Ratnakīrti and Ratnakāraśānti, which makes clear again that Ratnakīrti does not accept *antarvyāpti* and instead uses an arbitrary example (e.g., a pot) from outside the cases immediately at issue. He relies on a *prasaṅga,* or reductio argument, and its transformation into an ordinary inference to provide supporting argument to show that the example is indeed a similar case. Thus it provides evidence for pervasion between existence and momentariness (*Tarkabhāṣā* 47.1–18; Kajiyama, pp. 111–12). This confirms our translation of *prasaṅga-viparyaya* as "the transformation of a *prasaṅga* into an ordinary inference," and has proved indispensable for our understanding of the overall structure of Ratnakīrti's argument.

In a 1999 dissertation Jeson Woo undertakes a detailed comparison of all available publications and manuscripts of the text of *Kṣaṇabhaṅga-siddhi-Anvayātmikā*, produces a slightly improved version over A. Thakur's second edition (see below), and translates with explanatory notes.[19] Unfortunately we were not aware of this study until after we completed our translation based on Thakur's 1975 book. Woo also traces virtually every reference Ratnakīrti makes to his predecessors in the Buddhist tradition as well as to Nyāya opponents who voice the objections addressed by him in his text who are usually not explicitly referenced by him. With a wealth of historical contextualization, Woo's work complements ours, our aim being to explicate the argument itself with precision and clarity. To be sure, it is important to honor the inherited canons of epistemology and logic, but our purpose has been in part to make it all accessible to philosophers not versed in Indian traditions. Where we have included such information, however, we are usually indebted to Woo, who has done admirable digging in a host of Ratnakīrti's predecessors.

---

[18] Kajiyama (1998).

[19] Woo (1999).

3. The Text

A manuscript for the *Kṣaṇabhaṅgasiddhi* (*KBS*) was among a large number of palm-leaf manuscripts found by Mahāpaṇḍita Rāhula Sāṅkṛtyāyana in various monasteries in and around Tibet. The *KBS* manuscript was part of a bundle of manuscripts found in the Zhalu monastery. Photoprints were made from this bundle and the collection was provisionally entitled the *Ratnakīrtinibandhāḥ* by its discoverer. The photoprints consisted of eighty-six folia written in Maithil script from around 1200 CE. They contain twelve works, including the two parts of the *KBS* and two texts by Paṇḍita Aśoka.[20] Six of these works, including the two parts of the *KBS* were first edited by Haraprasāda Śāstrī, and published under the title *Six Buddhist Nyāya Tracts*.[21] In 1957, Anantalal Thakur edited the ten works by Ratnakīrti and published them under the title *Ratnakīrti-nibandhāvali: Buddhist Nyāya Works of Ratnakīrti*. Although Thakur notes that his manuscript for the second part frequently diverges from the Śāstrī version, Thakur's manuscript for the first part of the *KBS* largely agrees with Śāstrī's.[22] A second edition of Thakur's collection was published in 1975 and this is the manuscript upon which our translation is based. The transliteration of the text given here along with the translation and commentary mirrors this edition (except for obvious misprints). We do not indicate compounds by hyphens or break *sandhi*, nor do we use any special diacritical marks to indicate a vowel *sandhi* at the word junction of a compound. A period has been used to indicate the presence of a *daṇḍa*. We have indicated textual emendations in footnotes.

As noted, Jeson Woo also presents the text in transliteration. His constructions are "largely based on the second edition of A. Thakur" but incorporate an additional manuscript as well Thakur's sources.[23] Checking all the variant readings, which Woo conveniently lists, we find none that significantly alter the meaning. With perhaps one or two exceptions, the omission of an *iti* or *ādi* here and there and an occasional replacement by a synonym are the most major differences. Our punctuation, however,

[20] Thakur (1975), Introduction, pp. 1–2.

[21] Haraprasāda Śāstrī (1910).

[22] Thakur (1975), Introduction, p. 2, footnote 2.

[23] Woo (1999), p. 29.

in more than two dozen instances differs from Woo's commentary, from the paragraph breaks in Thakur.

4. On Translation

With regard to translation style, we have employed a maximalist strategy that is also in a way minimalist. Ratnakīrti's sentences are rendered in sentences with ellipses restored, propositional anaphora filled in with the propositions referred to, and background assumptions provided (in parentheses). Our aim has been to translate Ratnakīrti in sentences that read fluidly on the principle that as little as possible should be filled in (the minimalism) so long as a sentence is readable and makes plain Ratnakīrti's sense (the maximalism). Parentheses are used generously to indicate that a word or phrase has no explicit correlate in the Sanskrit or to supply a presupposition or to allow a quick gloss or rewording, not directly translating the text. If these practices are distracting or hard to keep in mind, please ignore the parentheses and treat their content as part of the text. This is sound advice because everything provided in English under the headings, "Text and Translation," including the longest expressions in parentheses, is to be understood as meant by Ratnakīrti's Sanskrit sentences. Admittedly, in some cases the line is hard to draw between the truly implicit which is so closely presupposed that without it a sentence could not be read—which we take to be subject to restoration in English—and elaboration and exegesis appropriate to commentary. As indicated, a running commentary is provided under the heading, "Comments," where more extensive explanations of background theories are presented as well as reconstructions of arguments. But the goal has been to make the translation intelligible without comments. One should be able to read the translation by itself, without relying on the comments at all.

Several liberal translational practices are utilized, such as squeezing verbs out of nominalizations, turning passive into active constructions, and rendering a single Sanskrit adjective with a pair of English adjectives or an adjectival phrase. Moreover, ellipsis is commonly restored, and antecedents commonly substituted in place of anaphoric pronouns. Ratnakīrti's Sanskrit can, nevertheless, be reconstructed or at least traced from the English. Thus, probably not much needs to be said in justification of these practices all done in the interest of intelligibility and readability. However, the discourse structure of classical philosophic texts, such as

Ratnakīrti's, which we make explicit by labeling speakers, may require defending for some.

Identifying the speaker explicitly and by concordant paragraph breaks are not stylistic features of Ratnakīrti's Sanskrit, but they are urged because of the complex dialectical organization of the text. Ratnakīrti defends his views—the position to be established (*siddhānta*)—against objections from an opponent (*pūrvapakṣin*). The opponent's views are presented in great detail and are themselves sometimes defended against the use of adverbial discourse markers, in particular, the paragraph adverbs, *nanu* and *atha*. Such terms need not be directly translated as their meaning may be absorbed into English paragraph breaks and disputant labeling. We thus label each passage as an objection, or an objection to an objection, or as being the voice of Ratnakīrti himself. This style is appropriate, we believe, although it cannot be denied that there is an interpretive element in discerning discourse structure. It is nonetheless absolutely necessary to know from whose perspective a thesis is advanced in order to follow the overall argumentation.

There are three other rules of translational and interpretive practice that we might briefly rehearse.

(1) The *principle of intelligibility*: A translator should not render what is intelligible in a source language as unintelligible in a target language. Different languages have different thresholds of tolerance for ellipsis, presupposition, anaphoric reference, and the like. Thus adherence to this principle often requires target constructions that are innovative.

(2) The *principle of readability*: Between two expressions with the same meaning, a translator should choose the more readable. This principle trumps any merit there might be in trying to mirror the syntax of the source or to use words in one-to-one correspondence. That is to say, this principle trumps what we might call misguided literalness.

(3) The *principle of charity*: A translator should choose the best interpretation, which is, for starters, a non-contradictory interpretation. We assume in conversation, debate, and so on, that a speaker would not, except in special circumstances, contradict himself or herself. Thus, without being able to provide a special explanation, we should not settle for an interpretation that is contradictory. An apparent contradiction makes us look for another interpretation, just as in everyday conversation we would either understand an apparent contradiction as a figure of speech or ask our interlocutor just what he or she means. The principle of charity

also demands we assume the sincerity of our author as a philosopher, a sense on his part of relevance, as well as, beyond non-contradiction, a sense of overall coherence. Indeed, we interpret a philosopher as trying, in any particular instance, to say something true and warranted as well as coherent with his or her overall view. Of course, such granting of trustworthiness to Ratnakīrti has to be contextualized. This means that with respect to his own times he would not deny, for example, a bit of world knowledge commonly assumed. At least we may presume he would not do so without somehow signaling the fact.

5. The Doctrine of Momentariness

The doctrine of momentariness has a long and interesting history in Buddhist thought. Though it is not present in the earliest strata of Buddhist literature, where the endurance of everyday objects for short periods of time is often assumed,[24] the doctrine emerges around the beginning of the common era in the Abhidharma literature, where the nature of the "*dharmas*," the fundamental elements that make up the world, is examined. The doctrine of momentariness seems to develop out of a logical extension of the early Buddhist principles of impermanence and no-self. A central principle of Buddhism from the beginning is that all conditioned things are impermanent. Originally, however, this seems to have implied merely that nothing lasts forever, not the much stronger claim that nothing lasts for more than a single moment.[25] In the Abhidharma literature, things are held to be mere collections of *dharmas*, with no underlying substance. Consequently, change of any kind involves the replacement of one *dharma* by another, rather than the modification of an enduring substratum. Moreover, the principle of impermanence is interpreted to mean that the collections are changing constantly. It follows that things are not only eventually destroyed, they change in some way at every moment. The combination of these two principles—that everything is a mere collection and that everything changes at every moment—implies that everything is momentary.

[24] For example, *Samyutta-Nikāya* II, 190–193; see Alexander von Rospatt (1995), p. 15.

[25] For example, *Samyutta-Nikāya* XII, 62; see Henry Clarke Warren (1963), pp. 150–152.

This first argument for momentariness, which Alexander Von Rospatt calls "the argument from change," seems to be the earliest argument in favor of the view and the line of reasoning that motivates its development.[26] Several other arguments are developed over the course of the next few centuries to defend the view against various objections from its Nyāya opponents. At least four kinds of argument in favor of momentariness can be found in the Buddhist literature, from:

1. Change
2. The momentariness of cognition
3. Spontaneous destruction
4. Causal efficiency

Advocates of momentariness come to make all four arguments.

The second argument targets cognition: things must be momentary because they are the causes of cognition, which is itself momentary. This argument depends on the questionable assumption that the causes of momentary things must be momentary, and the hidden assumption that the cognizer as well as cognition is momentary.

Some Buddhists also put forth a third argument based on the idea of spontaneous destruction. Things are momentary, they argue, because the destruction of a thing cannot be caused; it must occur spontaneously as a result of the thing's nature. Consequently, each thing must expire spontaneously as soon as it comes into existence, for its nature is already present. This argument depends on the controversial assumption that destruction cannot be caused by an outside force.[27] The opponents of momentariness criticized these first three arguments at length over the course of several hundred years from the third century to the seventh, and Buddhists continued to employ the three in various forms to defend their view.

The fourth and most sophisticated line of reasoning, the argument from causal efficiency, is first put forth by Dharmakīrti early in the eighth century.[28] This argument starts from the assumption that anything that

---

[26] Rospatt (1995), pp. 15–28.

[27] See Rospatt (1995) for a detailed discussion of the first three types of argument for momentariness.

[28] Dharmakīrti, *Hetubindu* 2.28. See Gokhale (1997), p. 50.

exists must have causal efficiency; it must be capable of producing an effect. Whatever the effect is, once it is produced, the thing that causes it can no longer have that capacity. Otherwise, it would go on producing that same effect again and again. Therefore, it must cease to exist immediately after it causes its effect. But since everything must have capacity at every moment it exists, everything must cease to exist immediately after the first moment it comes into being. This argument becomes the central focus of the momentariness debate after Dharmakīrti, and it is developed and defended by a series of Buddhist philosophers including Śāntarakṣita, Kamalaśīla, and Jñānaśrīmitra. It is this same line of reasoning that is carefully articulated and defended by Ratnakīrti in the *KBS*.

The most vocal opponents of the doctrine of momentariness over the centuries are members of the Nyāya school, including Vātsyāyana, Uddyotakara, Vācaspati Miśra, Trilocana, and Udayana. The Nyāya school rejects the Buddhist ontological analysis of the world in terms of collections of *dharmas*, holding that the world consists of substances that exist distinct from and independently of their various properties. Consequently, Nyāya philosophers hold that substances can endure through changes in properties. They therefore reject the doctrine of momentariness and are not convinced by the argument from change, which depends on rejecting any distinction between properties and property-bearers.[29] They also reject the argument from spontaneous destruction, insisting that having a destructible self-nature does not preclude things from enduring until an outside auxiliary condition arrives to trigger the destruction of the thing.[30] They reject the argument from causal efficiency on similar grounds, arguing that a thing can have the capacity to produce a certain effect, but not exercise that capacity until some other auxiliary condition is met and triggers it. From this it follows that things do not have to exhaust their capacity and expire immediately after they come into being. The issue of unrealized capacities thus becomes one of the main points of contention in the dispute between the Buddhists and the Naiyāyikas over

[29] Vātsyāyana, *Nyāyasūtrabhāṣya*. See Mrinalkanti Gangapodhyaya (1982). See especially 4.1.35–36 and 2.1.31–36. The Naiyāyikas also explicitly reject the claim that things change at every moment: see 3.2.10–14.

[30] Uddyotakara, *Nyāyavārtika* 3.2.14. See Ganganatha Jha (1919), pp. 1303–1324.

momentariness.[31] Ratnakīrti exerts considerable effort to show that there are no unrealized capacities.

The Naiyāyikas also offer an important argument of their own against momentariness, which Ratnakīrti considers in some detail in the *KBS*. The argument is based upon the phenomenon of recognition, the experience that an object that I observe now is the same object as one I previously experienced. Recognition is more than mere remembrance but the memory portion is supposed to prove endurance. Recognition depends on my being am the same observer who previously observed this same object that I am experiencing now. Nyāya philosophers point out that one person does not have another's memories.

In its most powerful formulation—which involves a "cross-modality" twist, combining two sensory modes—the cognition takes the form, "I am now touching what I previously saw." Here the Buddhist challenge of explaining the cognition becomes particularly difficult, since each sense organ is viewed as restricted to its own object range, and a later cognition of texture cannot even be imagined to belong to the cognizer of the previous cognition which is visual. Nor is it clear how the two cognitions could be imagined to be of the same object. However, there is the rule that conventional speech reflecting common experience, *vyavahāra*, gets prima facie weight, and "I am now touching what I previously saw" is conventional.

In a nutshell, Naiyāyikas argue that recognition would be impossible if everything were momentary; recognition proves both that the cognizer and the object must be capable of enduring at least as long as the time between the two cognitions.[32] The Buddhists, for their part, must argue that this experience is a mistaken cognition, resulting from a failure to distinguish things that are distinct. It requires quite a bit of ingenuity, however, to give this account. The Buddhist must show that the information from the earlier cognition can be made available to the later cognizer and that the information can be mistakenly incorporated into a cognition of identity where there is none. Ratnakīrti addresses the argument

---

[31] Udayana, *Ātmatattvaviveka*. See N.S. Dravid (1995), pp. 9–42. See also Joy Laine (1998).

[32] For further discussion of this argument, see Kisor Chakrabarti (1999), pp. 93–113. See also Arindam Chakrabarti (1992) and Ganeri (2000).

at length in his *Sthīrasiddhidūṣaṇa*, where he develops an account of recognition entirely on the basis of momentary entities. But he also considers the issue in the *KBS*, where he offers an abridged version of his reasoning.

6. The Inferential Pattern

By the time of Ratnakīrti, the arguments on both sides of the momentariness debate had become quite complex, and our philosopher painstakingly reconstructs his argument along with responses to various objections according to an inferential pattern shared by both Buddhists and non-Buddhists. The pattern was put forth in various schools and texts usually as part of a theory of knowledge that, in each school, became progressively quite technical and elaborate, with strict rules governing the justification of a claim and an extensive list of flaws and fallacies that could undermine a proposed justification. The intricate structure of Ratnakīrti's argument involves several iterations of a basic inferential pattern. The various objections he considers and responses he makes must also be understood in terms of the various fallacies and flaws to which such inferences are subject, according to the common logical inheritance. We must therefore carefully examine in particular the basic inferential pattern and keep it mind as we proceed through Ratnakīrti's text along with the general debate theory and epistemologies which it informs.

The central concept in all classical Indian epistemology is *pramāṇa*, "knowledge source" and (given doubt or controversy) "means of justification." A cognition is considered knowledge only if it is produced by a process that guarantees its truth. Such a process is a means of justification because it is capable of dispelling doubt about a claim that is the subject of a dispute. Some Buddhist philosophers, most notably Nāgārjuna, reject the *pramāṇa* theory of knowledge, but a long Buddhist tradition which includes Vasubandhu, Dignāga, and Dharmakīrti accepts the *pramāṇa* approach. Ratnakīrti belongs to this lineage and wholeheartedly embraces the principle that there are identifiable processes whose employment and results can serve as justification for knowledge claims.

The Buddhist and Nyāya schools disagree over the number and definitions of the *pramāṇas*, but they are in broad agreement that both perception and inference are *pramāṇas*. Dignāga, the first systematizer of Buddhist epistemology, identifies two *pramāṇas*: direct knowledge, i.e., perception, and indirect knowledge, i.e., knowledge through a sign. The

Buddhists and their Nyāya opponents differ in their definitions of perception, but they both accept it as a knowledge source and justifier. Dignāga defines perception as a cognition completely free of conceptual construction. Direct perception is consequently always indeterminate and any determinate perception involves an element of indirect knowledge.[33] The Nyāya school defines perception as a definite cognition that results from connection between a sense organ and an object.[34] Indirect knowledge for Dignāga includes not only inference, but also testimony and analogy. The Nyāya school distinguishes these three as separate *pramāṇas*. But both parties agree that knowledge obtained by perception, inference, testimony, and analogy is trustworthy. For our purposes, inference is the most important of these knowledge means because Ratnakīrti's arguments are framed in terms of inferential patterns, but perception is also relevant because inference as a *pramāṇa* (i.e., as generating knowledge of the world) depends in certain ways upon perception.

Indirect knowledge, according to Dignāga, proceeds on the basis of a sign (*liṅga*). In the case of inference, the sign is the prover (*hetu*), which indicates the presence of the probandum (*sādhya*) in the inferential subject (*pakṣa*). By means of an inference one gains a cognition of the inferential subject as qualified by the probandum. The cognition arises as a result of a prior cognition that the inferential subject is qualified by the prover along with the knowledge that everywhere the prover is found the probandum is also found. All this is traditionally presented according to a five-step inferential pattern capturing "inference for others" (*parārtha*) although "inference for oneself" (*svārtha*) may be simpler, requiring only two or three steps. Here is the five-step pattern used in formal debates illustrated by a stock example, knowledge of fire from a perception of smoke:

1. The mountain is fiery.
2. Because it is smoky.
3. Whatever is smoky is fiery.
4. The mountain is an example of something smoky.
5. Therefore the mountain is fiery.

---

33 Dignāga, *Pramāṇasamuccaya*. See Hattori (1968), pp. 24–32.

34 Vātsyāyana, *Nyāyasūtrabhāṣya* 1.1.4. See Gangapodhyaya (1982), pp. 14–16.

The first step is the statement of the hypothesis (*pratijñā*) to be proved by the inference. The second step states the grounds (*hetu*) from which the conclusion follows by pointing out that the locus or subject at issue is qualified by the prover. The third step asserts a universal pervasion (*vyāpti*) between the prover and the probandum. The fourth step merely reiterates that the subject, being qualified by the prover, falls under the general rule stated in (3). The fifth step restates the hypothesis from (1) as following from the other steps.[35]

An inference of this sort is thus in fact based upon two premises, a premise stating that a locus or subject at issue possesses the prover and a premise stating a pervasion between prover and probandum:

1. There is smoke on the mountain.
2. Everywhere there is smoke, there is fire.
3. Therefore there is fire on the mountain.

An argument of this form is obviously formally valid, so the only question we typically face is the acceptability of the premises. In a good inference as understood by classical Indian philosophers across schools (though some in late Nyāya might disagree), the premises must not only be true, but they must be known. Therefore they must have been produced by a *pramāṇa*. The first premise in the stock example is considered uncontroversially supported by perception. My cognition that there is smoke on the mountain is acceptable because I see it. It could of course be supported by testimony or even another inference, but somewhere along the line a perception must support the first premise. The second premise is also supported by perception, because it is mainly by cognition of examples where it is known that the prover and the probandum are found together that a cognition of a universal pervasion is formed. For instance, in our example, observation of smoke and fire together in a kitchen hearth contributes to the generation of a cognition of a universal pervasion between smoke and fire. These supporting examples may also be justified by another inference or by testimony, but any chain of inference, or testimony, must eventually end in direct perception.

Our stock inferential pattern is usually found in an abbreviated form and Ratnakīrti follows the convention. The short form proceeds by stating

[35] *Nyāyasūtra* 1.1.33–39. See also S. C. Chatterjee (1939), pp. 299–301.

that the inferential subject is qualified by the probandum because it is qualified by the prover. To this is added a known example of something possessing the prover which also possesses the probandum. For example:

> The mountain is fiery because it is smoky, like the kitchen hearth.

Here the pervasion is not stated directly, but is indicated by the example. The example serves not just to illustrate the general rule, but to provide some basis of support for the generalization.

Dignāga held that a sign must meet three conditions to serve as the basis of a sound inference:

1. Presence in the inferential subject (*pakṣa*).
2. Presence in at least one similar case (*sapakṣa*).
3. Absence in any dissimilar case (*vipakṣa*).

The first condition ensures that the prover qualifies the locus where the probandum is to be inferred. The second condition demands at least one positive correlation between the prover and the probandum. A single positive example is all the positive evidence needed in certain circumstances to establish the pervasion between the prover and the probandum (that is, on a principle of defeasibility). The third condition demands that there be no counterexamples. This is a broad condition because the prover must be known to be absent from all cases where the probandum is absent. The second and third conditions jointly establish the pervasion in normal cases. In the case of smoke and fire, we must have at least one positive example of smoke and fire together (e.g., the kitchen hearth). There must also be no place without fire where there is smoke (e.g., smoke's absence in water is required by the absence of fire). When all three conditions are met, the presence of the probandum in the subject at issue is established by inference.[36]

There is some dispute over the necessity of both the second and the third conditions. It could be argued that (1) and (3) are sufficient for the inference to be sound. The third condition establishes a negative (*vyatireka*) correlation between the prover and the probandum, whose expression (B is absent wherever A is absent) is equivalent to its contrapositive (wherever

---

[36] For a detailed account of the inferential pattern see Matilal (1998), pp. 89–111.

A is present, B is present). Therefore the pervasion can be established entirely by negative correlation. However, there remains the possibility that, even though the prover does not occur in any dissimilar cases, it also does not occur in any similar cases, because it does not occur outside of the inferential subject at all. For this reason, Dignāga includes the second condition, demanding that at least one positive example be cited to support the pervasion even when a negative correlation is already established. The Nyāya school, on the other hand, drops the second condition in situations where there are no similar cases at all. But where there are similar cases, such inferences are rejected as lacking support from positive examples (*asādhāraṇa*). Later Buddhists including Ratnakīrti accepted such inferences in situations where there are no similar cases.[37]

The distinction between positive and negative correlation becomes crucial for understanding Ratnakīrti's argument, because he frequently relies on it. Indeed, the division of the text into two parts is based on it. The distinction generates a three-fold division among inferences:

1. Positive Correlation Only (*kevalānvaya*)
2. Negative Correlation Only (*kevalavyatireka*)
3. Positive and Negative Correlation (*anvayavyatireka*)

In the first part of Ratnakīrti's text, which is translated in the present work, he gives an inference of the first type, i.e., based upon positive correlations (*anvaya*): everything that exists is momentary. In the second part, he gives an inference of the second type, i.e., based upon negative correlations (*vyatireka*): everything that is non-momentary is non-existent. Even in the first part of the *KBS*, however, Ratnakīrti frequently adopts the *vyatireka* mode in order to establish one or another supporting inference, relying on the law of transposition to ensure that the negative correlation alone is sufficient to establish the pervasions.

Another important way of classifying inferences is by the nature of the relation between the prover and the probandum. Dharmakīrti distinguishes three types of inference, involving three different types of prover,

---

[37] For more on the alleged redundancy of the second condition, see Bhatt and Mehrotra (2000), pp. 79–84.

each of which is based on a different kind of necessary relationship between the prover and the probandum.[38]

1. Identity (*svabhāva-hetu*)
2. Causal Relationship (*kārya-hetu*)
3. Non-apprehension (*anupalabhi-hetu*)

The familiar example of the pervasion between smoke and fire is an example of an inference based on *kārya-hetu*. Fire is a necessary causal condition for the occurrence of smoke. Consequently, wherever there is smoke, there is fire. The causal relationship is a relationship between each particular smoke and each particular fire. The empirical evidence supports the fact that this relationship actually exists.

The third type of prover is the non-apprehension of a thing that is perceptible. For instance, although a pot is perceptible, if one is not seen, it may be inferred that one is not present. Dharmakīrti treats this case as an inference in order to avoid having to attribute the knowledge to perception of an absence or of a bare locus (the views of Nyāya and Mīmāṃsā respectively). Positing absences as distinct entities is considered ontologically extravagant by Buddhists, and the perception of the bare locus by itself seems insufficient to account for the cognition that there is no pot there. Dharmakīrti thus classifies it as a distinct type of inference.

The most important of the three types for our purposes is *svabhāva-hetu*, because Ratnakīrti's argument for momentariness is of this type. Indeed, when Dharmakīrti explains this type of inference in his *Hetubindu*, he uses the argument for momentariness as an illustration. A *svabhāva-hetu* inference has a prover whose own nature includes the probandum. For example:

> This is a tree, because it is an oak.

The probandum, being a tree, is inferred from the prover, being an oak. This type of inference operates on the basis of a relationship of identity (*tādātmya*). There is a universal pervasion between being an oak and being a tree. The identity relationship is a relationship a particular bears to itself; an oak is a tree by its very nature. This relationship does not need

---

[38] Dharmakīrti, *Hetubindu*. See Gokhale (1997), p. 14. See also Matilal (1998), pp. 111–116.

to be supported by empirical examples: it is a truth known from merely understanding the meanings of "tree" and "oak." We cite an empirical example merely to conform to the formal requirements of inference, and to draw attention to the relation to someone who may not notice it. The argument for momentariness depends upon a pervasion of this type. Our overall interpretation is that Ratnakīrti holds that the pervasion upon which his inference depends is a conceptual truth following from an analysis of the concepts of momentariness, existence, and causal efficiency.

An opponent can argue against an inference in a wide variety of ways. If any of the conditions for a true knowledge-generating inference are not met, the inference is rightly rejected. There is a long list of fallacies corresponding to the various ways an inference can fail to meet the requirements for knowledge-generation. There are also other ways putative inferences can be defeated by an opponent. These fallacies are organized in various ways by different schools on the Indian scene, but despite some minor disagreements Ratnakīrti and his Nyāya opponents largely agree on what counts as a legitimate defeater for an inference put forth in a philosophic debate or inquiry.

The most important flaws that affect inferences are the *hetvābhāsa*s (pseudo-provers). These are types of provers that look like they meet the conditions for making the inference sound, but which fail in various ways. The most important of the various fallacies are as follows—at least Ratnakīrti generally frames his objections and responses in terms of these three broad types of fallacy identified early in his text:

1. The unwarranted (*asiddha*)
2. The inconclusive (*anaikāntika*)
3. The contradictory (*viruddha*)

A prover is unwarranted when there is no evidence that it qualifies the case at issue, thus violating Dignāga's first condition. The prover is also unwarranted if it implies something contradictory to the nature of the inferential subject. For instance, if the inferential subject in our standard example is not a mountain, but a lake, then an inference that the lake is on fire produces a contradiction with the known nature of the lake (which cannot burn). In such a case the prover is unwarranted because of its own nature (*svarūpāsiddha*). If the prover is asserted to be present in a locus that is non-existent, then the prover is unwarranted in its basis (*āśrayāsiddha*). The Nyāya school lodges this charge against the *vyatireka* form of Ratnakīrti's inference: everything that is non-momentary does not exist. How, they ask, can non-existent things be used as supporting examples for an inference? Ratnakīrti expends much effort in the second part of the *KBS* defending his argument against this charge.

A prover is inconclusive when there are undisputed counterexamples where the probandum occurs without the prover, in violation of Dignāga's second and/or third conditions. If there is a clear-cut case of smoke without fire, then we must admit there is no pervasion and all of our inferences based on it must be repudiated. The counterexample, of course, cannot be among the cases at issue (*pakṣa*) without begging the question. It would not be acceptable to offer the smoke on the mountain as a counterexample to the pervasion between smoke and fire! The proponent, of course, can always dispute the claim that a so-called counterexample really is a similar case (*sapakṣa*). For instance, the inference cannot be shown to be inconclusive by citing fog as a kind of smoke without fire, because fog is not smoke. A proponent can also dispute the claim that the probandum really is absent in a putative counterexample. For instance, a recently extinguished campfire where there is smoke without fire seems to be counterexample, but a proponent can argue (as would almost all on the classical Indian scene) that there is fire in the smoldering embers even when there is no visible flame.

Finally, a prover is contradictory when it proves the opposite of what is intended. For instance, the inference of fire from water is contradictory because where there is water, there is no fire.

Sometimes, when no undisputed counterexample is available, a prover can be shown to be inconclusive by means of an inferential undercutter (*upādhi*). An inferential undercutter is a property which is possessed by everything that has the prover quality but not everything that has the quality to be proved. If such a property exists, a counterexample can be inferred. For instance, the use of fire as a prover for smoke is inconclusive. The pervasion does not hold because not everything fiery is smoky. For instance, a ball of hot iron is not smoky though it is fiery. The prover could be shown to be inconclusive by the inferential undercutter, wet fuel. Everything that is smoky has wet fuel, but there are some fiery things without wet fuel. This shows that there is a counterexample, though we may not have a specific example.

An inference can also be undermined by a counter-inference (*satpratipakṣa*) proving the opposite conclusion. Another flaw is a prover that is unsupported (*anupasamhāri*). Here there would be neither similar cases (*sapakṣa*) nor dissimilar cases (*vipakṣa*), and so there would be no basis for either assertion or denial of pervasion. We have already mentioned the flaw of having no supporting example (*asādhāraṇa*). This occurs when a *vyatireka*-only inference is given in a situation where known similar cases exist and so should be cited. There are other fallacies and points of defeat, but these should suffice for appreciating the fact that they feed the dialectic structure of Ratnakīrti's text. We shall elaborate some of them further, along with one or two others, in comments where appropriate.[39]

7. Ratnakīrti's Argument in the *KBS* Anvayātmikā

Ratnakīrti's argument for momentariness is laid out in the first few pages of the text, and the rest of the text is devoted to replying to various objections. The argument is complex in structure, consisting of a main inference supported by several layers of supporting inferences. All of these inferences can be formally reconstructed, and we shall proceed by spelling out each inference in three-step form, identifying the inferential subject, the prover, the probandum, as well as the supporting example.

Ratnakīrti frames his main inference as a proof of momentariness from existence, citing an arbitrary object as the supporting example. He then proceeds to demonstrate that the example is itself momentary by offering a supporting argument which depends on the further premise that to exist is to be capable of producing an effect. Further inferences are adduced to show that capacity implies momentariness and in this way Ratnakīrti is able to provide support for his main inference from existence.

The main inference is given in the first few sentences: "What exists is momentary, like a pot. And these things which have become the subject of dispute are existent" (below, under the heading, *Text and Translation* p. 67, lines 6–7). The argument can be reconstructed as follows:

1. The subjects under dispute exist.
2. Whatever exists is momentary, like a pot.
3. Therefore, the subjects under dispute are momentary.

---

[39] *Nyāyasūtra* 1.2.5–8. See Gangopadhyaya (1982), pp. 56–60. See also Chatterjee (1939), pp. 309–316.

Here the inferential subject is whatever is under dispute between the Buddhists and their opponents. The Nyāya school, for instance, holds that there are numerous entities that are permanent, including the self, atoms, and space. They also hold that most composite entities, though impermanent, endure for much longer than a moment. They do admit that certain entities such as flames and cognitions are momentary, but everything else that exists is at issue in this debate. Indeed, the inferential subject could be taken to include everything that exists, since the argument purports to establish momentariness universally. However, this would be problematic because all possible supporting examples, such as the pot, would be included in the inferential subject, leaving Ratnakīrti open to the charge that his inference suffers from the flaw of being without supporting examples (*asādhāraṇa*). As we shall see, Ratnakīrti runs into this problem on either interpretation of "inferential subject," because the pot becomes a subject of dispute in either case. Ratnakīrti does not resort to the method of drawing examples from within the inferential subject (*antarvyāpti*) as Ratnakaraśānti does, possibly because this move is not allowed according to the Nyāya adversary. Instead, Ratnakīrti leaves the expression for the inferential subject initially ambiguous, identifying it merely as the set of things that are under dispute. He then takes the pot as the supporting example treating it as lying outside of the inferential subject, but he immediately acknowledges that the opponent will dispute the example and that a further argument will thus be needed to show that the pot is momentary.

The prover of the main inference is existence (*sattva*), and since we are arguing only about things that everyone agrees exists, everything in the inferential subject is accepted by all parties to be qualified by the prover. The probandum is momentariness, and the pervasion is stated in (2): Everything that is qualified by existence is also qualified by momentariness. The supporting example is the pot, which Ratnakīrti contends is both existent and momentary.

One might ask at this stage why Ratnakīrti chooses a pot as his supporting example, rather than something accepted by his opponents as momentary such as a flame. Obviously, the example is not going to be at all convincing to an opponent, who will simply dispute the claim that the example is qualified by the probandum. But Ratnakīrti does not intend to demonstrate the momentariness of all things based upon an empirical example, such as a flame. If he proceeded in that way, his opponent would rightly be able to argue that his prover was inconclusive; there are many things other than flames, and they are not necessarily momentary just because flames are. Ratnakīrti intends to show that all existent things are momentary by showing that momentariness is embedded in the very concept of existence, when existence is understood correctly. He thus proceeds by choosing an arbitrary example, about which he assumes nothing other than that it exists, much as a mathematician might choose an arbitrary triangle assuming only that is a right triangle in order to prove the Pythagorean theorem. This strategy accounts in part for the complexity of the structure of the overall argument. Most of the force of the argument is relegated to the supporting inferences, where Ratnakīrti proceeds to prove on independent grounds that the pot must be understood to be momentary as long as we understand it to exist.

Ratnakīrti then shifts his attention to the pot, taking it as the inferential subject of the supporting inferences, which he says have "the character of a *prasaṅga* and its transformation (*prasaṅgaprasaṅgaviparyaya*)." A *prasaṅga* is an untoward consequence that follows from a view which one seeks to refute; it is a kind of a reductio argument. Ratnakīrti intends to show the view that the pot is non-momentary leads to a sequence of absurd consequences. Each of these absurd consequences also can be transformed into a fully formed inference. There are two *prasaṅgas*, the second supporting the argument offered by the first, which in turn supports the conclusion that the pot is momentary. We will reconstruct each of these arguments and explicate the relationship between them.

A first absurd consequence can be drawn out once we understand the nature of existence as causal capacity. Ratnakīrti defines existence as "the capacity to produce an effect (*arthakriyākāritvam*)" (*Text and Translation* p. 67, lines 10–16). Given this definition, at any given moment, the pot must have the capacity to produce some effect. The untoward consequence is that if the pot endures for another moment it will be both capable and incapable of producing its future effect in the present moment. This follows because there are three possibilities if the pot endures. In the next moment, it can be capable of producing (1) the same effect, (2) the different effect, or (3) no effect at all. Option (3) is ruled out because the pot next moment, it can be capable of producing (1) the same effect, (2) a different exists *ex hypothesi* and by definition an existent thing must produce some effect. Option (1) is also impossible because one cannot produce what has already come to be. In fact, Ratnakīrti argues (*Text and Translation* p. 68, lines 1–16), the pot must produce a different effect in the next moment.

But in that case it has a different capacity, and since capacity is part of the very self-nature (*svabhāva*) of a thing, the later pot must be distinct from the earlier pot. Otherwise, the bad consequence follows immediately that it both has and does not have the capacity to produce its future effects in the present moment. For if it is the same thing in the future, it must have already had the capacity to produce those effects in the present moment, even though we can see that it does not produce those effects.

This *prasaṅga* can be transformed into the following inference:

1. The pot at the present moment does not produce the future effects.
2. What does not produce a given effect, is distinct from what does.
3. Therefore, the pot at the present moment is distinct from any future producer.

Here the inferential subject is the pot at the present moment, the prover is the non-production of the future effects, and the probandum is being distinct from the pot in the future moment. The first premise is an observed fact about the pot. The second premise follows from the fact that a single thing cannot bear contrary properties, especially properties that are as essential to self-nature as capacities are. It follows that the pot must be distinct from anything that is capable of producing those future effects. Consequently, the pot can endure for no more than a single moment. Later (*Text and Translation* pp. 78–79), the opponent will object to premise (2), and Ratnakīrti will give an argument to support it. But he is more concerned at this stage to cut off another objection, namely, that a thing can be capable of producing an effect in the future even though it does not produce that effect in the present moment. Ratnakīrti puts forth his next inference to head off that objection.

The issue of whether there can be unrealized capacities—and indeed the nature of causality itself—becomes central to the debate over momentariness because the argument proceeds from an analysis of what it means to be capable of producing an effect. As we shall see, the debate will turn on small details in our account of the process of causation. But at this point (*Text and Translation* p. 68, lines 17–19), Ratnakīrti offers another *prasaṅga* and a corresponding inference to show that to have capacity means to produce immediately. The bad consequence that follows if we deny this is that things will be worthy of being called capable even if they do not produce.

Ratnakīrti formally reconstructs this next inference as follows:

1. The pot now is appropriately spoken of as producing its future effects.
2. Whatever is appropriately said to be capable of producing *x*, produces *x*.
3. Therefore, the pot now produces its future effects.

The inferential subject here again is the pot at the present moment, the prover is its being appropriately called capable of producing its future effects, and the probandum is the production of those future effects. The first premise is the assumption of the opponent that there can be unrealized capacities. The conclusion supports the previous bad consequence that Ratnakīrti purports to show follows from an assumption that the pot endures. The pervasion stated in the second premise is supported by the example of the total collection of causal factors (*sāmagrī*) which the by both parties to be rightly said to be both capable and immediately Nyāya school regards as the immediate producer of an effect. This is agreed productive.

The opponent offers a seed as a counterexample to the pervasion claimed in the second premise (*Text and Translation* p. 68, lines 25–26). The seed is rightly said to be capable of producing a sprout, although it awaits water, soil, light, etc., to actually produce it. Therefore, there are some things that have the capacity to produce an effect even though they require some further auxiliary cause that has not yet arrived before they actually produce.

The discussion of auxiliary causality becomes quite intricate when Ratnakīrti defends his account of causation (*Text and Translation,* pp. 74–77). But at this point (*Text and Translation,* p. 68, lines 26–30), he simply offers an alternative explanation for why we speak in that way about the seed. He distinguishes between a literal and a metaphorical sense of "capable." In the metaphorical sense, he admits, the seed in the granary may rightly be called a producer of the future sprout, because it is the cause of the cause (etc.) in that it produces a successor seed. That successor through a chain of other successors produces the sprout. But the literal producer of the sprout is only that later seed that exists in conjunction with the other so-called auxiliary factors such as soil, water, light, etc. It is the literal sense of capacity we have in mind when we define existence as capacity to produce an effect, because it is literal capacity that is part of the inherent self-nature of a thing. For this reason, the seed cannot provide an undisputable counterexample to the pervasion of this inference.

Furthermore, Ratnakīrti insists (*Text and Translation* p. 69, lines 1–4), the inference does not leave any room for doubt regarding the negative form of the pervasion, namely, that all things that do not produce *x* at a given time are not correctly said to be capable of producing *x* at that time. First, he argues, the denial of this pervasion leads to the unfortunate consequence that there would be no restriction to speech regarding production and capacity. Anything could be said to produce anything, simply because the absence of other auxiliary factors could always be assumed to account for the non-production of the effect. For instance, a cat could be correctly said to be capable of speech because if it were given a human brain, vocal system, etc., it would actually produce speech. It is unclear why we should not regard these as auxiliary factors, just as soil and water are auxiliary factors for seeds. It would not be convincing to say that in the case of the cat those factors are unlikely to appear. For the seed also might never be planted, yet the opponent insists it is always capable. Hence, we must stick to the literal sense of capacity and accept the negative form of the pervasion to avoid a complete breakdown of our ability to make a meaningful linguistic distinction between the capable and incapable.

Ratnakīrti also transforms this *prasaṅga* into an inference (*Text and Translation* p. 69, lines 5–10), taking the pot at the present moment again as the inferential subject, the non-production of the effects as the prover, and not being appropriately called capable as the probandum. He formally reconstructs the inference as follows:

1. The pot at the present moment does not produce the future effects.
2. Whatever does not produce *x*, is not rightly called capable of producing *x*.
3. Therefore, the pot now is not appropriately spoken of as capable of its future effects.

The first premise here is the observed fact that the pot does not produce its future effects. The conclusion is that the pot should not be regarded as capable of producing those effects. This supports Ratnakīrti's contention that a contradiction follows if the pot endures, because it shows that the pot is not capable of producing its future effects, although it must be if it has the same self-nature as it has later.

The second premise here states the negative (*vyatireka*) form of the pervasion, about which Ratnakīrti wishes to show there is no doubt. Ratnakīrti offers an example to establish the pervasion, namely a barley seed which is not at the present moment rightly spoken of as capable of producing a rice sprout and does not in fact produce a rice sprout at the present moment. The opponent might try to counter that the prover is inconclusive because there is a counterexample: the rice seed in the granary is rightly spoken of as capable and it does not produce right now. However, this will not be a convincing objection, because Ratnakīrti will insist that the rice seed in the granary does not deserve to be called capable either and so it too becomes part of the inferential subject under dispute. The barley seed, however, is agreed by everyone to be undeserving to be called capable, so it remains available as evidence. In this way, the *vyatireka* form of the inference supports Ratnakīrti's pervasion and turns out to be supportable by concrete and undisputable empirical examples and free of any possible undisputable counterexamples.

Ratnakīrti also argues (*Text and Translation* p. 70, lines 17–28) that the positive and negative forms of a pervasion are equivalent. By the law of transposition, "All F are G" is equivalent to its contrapositive, "All non-G are non-F." Therefore, once either the negative or positive form of the pervasion is established there need be no doubt about the other.

We can now reconstruct Ratnakīrti's whole argument, revealing the various premises and assumptions and their inferential relationships as follows:

1. All the subjects under dispute exist.
2. Whatever exists is momentary, like a pot.
3. Anything that exists is capable of producing some effect (by definition).
4. At any given moment the pot is capable of producing an effect (from 3).
5. Anything rightly called capable produces immediately, like the *sāmagrī* (set of things together sufficient for an effect).
6. The pot is not capable of producing future effects in the present (from 5).

7. Whatever is not capable of producing x is distinct from what is.
8. The pot in the future is distinct from the pot in the present (from 6 and 7).
9. Therefore the pot is momentary (from 8).
10. Therefore, all things that exist are momentary (from 1, 2, and 9).

The first premise states simply that the items under dispute all exist. If the dispute extends to all things that exist, then the inferential subject is everything that is existent (*sat*). The contention that all these things exhibit existence (*sattva*), the prover property, is uncontroversial in either case. Premise (3) is a definition, and while it might be cause for some worry, it was not generally one of the points disputed by other schools. In any case, it hardly seems controversial to require that things that actually exist should be capable of demonstrating their existence by having some impact on the world. Otherwise, the water imagined in the mirage could be regarded as existing, even though it is incapable of quenching thirst. Premises (2), (5), and (7) assert universal pervasions, pervasions accepted by Ratnakīrti and company but elsewhere not. Our philosopher offers the example of the pot as evidence to support (2), which is obviously unconvincing by itself. But the premise is established if premises (3–8) successfully demonstrate the momentariness of the pot. Consequently, the weight of the argument overall and therefore the focus of the controversy lies with premises (5) and (7).

Since the other premises all follow logically from previous premises as indicated, the only remaining points of contention (aside from worries about the definition of existence) are premises (5) and (7). These comprise two of four big objections Ratnakīrti considers in the remainder of the text. Premise (5), requiring that anything worthy of being called capable produce immediately, is supported by the example of the *sāmagrī*, which everyone agrees is both capable and immediately productive. This example, however, remains controversial because the opponent will maintain that there is a good counterexample, namely, the seed. Ratnakīrti tries to defeat the counterexample by drawing a distinction between literal and metaphorical capacity, but this maneuver remains controversial. He also responds by supporting premise (5) in its negative form with the example of the barley seed which is not worthy of being called capable of producing a rice sprout and does not produce a rice sprout. This example is better, because it is undisputed and any counterexample the opponent could offer would be easily disputable by Ratnakīrti. Later, this premise becomes the focus of a long series of objections (*Text and Translation* pp. 74–77).

Premise (7) is supported by the argument that if capacity is part of a thing's self-nature then to lose a capacity is tantamount to destruction of the entity. This also becomes the subject of a closely argued series of objections (*Text and Translation* pp. 78–79).

The remainder of the text is devoted to four main objections to the theory of momentariness and Ratnakīrti's argument:

1. Recognition is impossible without an enduring self (*Text and Translation* pp. 71–74).
2. Auxiliary causes allow unrealized capacities (*Text and Translation* pp. 74–77).
3. Contrary properties do not imply distinctness (*Text and Translation* pp. 78–79).
4. Problems related to dependence and unity (*Text and Translation* pp. 80–82).

Objections 2 and 3 are related to the two controversial premises mentioned above, and Ratnakīrti in each case offers further argumentation. Objection 4 brings up further problems surrounding causation, most notably that of explaining how multiple causes can produce a single effect. In his response, Ratnakīrti develops an account of cooperative causation.

Objection 1 is intended to show that recognition is only possible on the assumption that there is an enduring subject capable of experiencing the same enduring object on two different occasions. This is a kind of counterinference showing the thesis of momentariness to be false. It would also undermine Ratnakīrti's argument in two ways. First, the opponent argues that without recognition there can be no awareness of causality, because the same person could never witness both the cause and the effect. This threatens to undermine the whole argument by making it impossible to rely on an analysis of causal relations. Second, the opponent argues that without recognition there can be no grasping of a pervasion, which requires many individual observations of the prover and the probandum together. If the opponent is right on this count, inference itself would be impossible if the thesis of universal momentariness were correct. And obviously if there can be no inference, there can be no proof of momentariness. The first objection thus poses significant challenges to Ratnakīrti's argument. He addresses it, we shall see, by offering an account of recognition that does not assume the existence of any non-momentary entities.

PART TWO

Annotated English Translation of Ratnakīrti's Kṣaṇabhaṅgasiddhi Anvayātmikā

Namas Tārāyai.
Homage to Tārā.

Text and Translation (p. 67, lines 4–5)

ākṣiptavyatirekā yā vyāptir anvayarūpiṇī. sādharmyavati dṛṣṭānte sattvahetor ihocyate.

The (inference-supporting) pervasion, whose negative form is implied, is here said to have the form of positive correlation, because, given that the example shows similarity, the prover is existence.

Comments

As explained in the introduction, every inference depends upon a pervasion (*vyāpti*) between the prover (*hetu*) and the probandum (*sādhya*), that is to say, everything that possesses the prover quality also possesses the probandum. There are two forms in which a pervasion may be stated to reflect the sort of evidence that supports it. Similarly, there are two forms of inference. Inferences in the form of positive correlation (*anvaya*) depend upon evidence that the probandum occurs everywhere the prover occurs. An inference in the form of negative correlations (*vyatireka*) depends upon evidence that the prover is absent wherever the probandum is absent. A pervasion in the form of negative correlation is expressed by the contrapositive of the expression of the positive pervasion. For instance, the negative form of the inference of fire from smoke depends on our knowing that everywhere that fire is not found, smoke is not found either. It follows from this that if there is smoke on the mountain, there is fire there too, since a proposition is equivalent to its contrapositive by the law of transposition. Ratnakīrti stresses the equivalence between the negative and positive forms because his argument cannot be supported by negative correlations: his prover is existence and so any example supporting the negative correlation would be non-existent. In the second half of the text, Ratnakīrti examines peculiar problems facing the negative form of the inference from existence.[40] We will, however, encounter inferences based on both positive and negative correlations even in this first section, and

[40] As noted, McDermott (1969) is a translation of the *Vyatirekātmikā*.

Ratnakīrti will rely on the equivalence of the two forms when it becomes difficult to support the negative form directly with examples.

Text and Translation (p. 67, lines 6–7)

> *yat sat tat kṣaṇikam. yathā ghaṭaḥ. santaś cāmī vivādāspadībhūtāḥ padārthā iti.*

What exists is momentary. Like a pot. And these things which have become the subject of dispute are existent.

Comments

The pervasion is stated in the first sentence. Whatever has existence (*sattva*) also possesses momentariness (*kṣaṇikatva*). The second sentence gives the example, a pot, which is both existent and momentary. The third sentence indicates that the inferential subject (*pakṣa*) is things whose endurance is under dispute. In any inference, the *pakṣa* is the locus where the probandum is proved by force of the presence of the prover. In the terms of the stock example, the mountain is the *pakṣa*. A necessary condition governing inference is *pakṣadharmatā*: the *pakṣa* must be characterized by, or qualified by, the prover. The mountain must be smoky if we are to infer that it is fiery. A second condition is that the relationship between the prover and probandum terms be universal. The Buddhist claims that things that the opponent contends endure are without exception momentary.

The example of the pot supports the pervasion claimed in the first sentence. Since the opponent will insist that that the pot too is under dispute and so cannot be used as an example, Ratnakīrti will offer another inference to show that the pot is momentary. Thus it will be shown to be evidence of a positive correlation between existence and momentariness. This supporting inference, which is based upon causal efficiency, is really the heart of Ratnakīrti's argument, as we will see.

Text and Translation (p. 67, lines 8–9)

> *hetoḥ parokṣārthapratipādakatvaṃ hetvābhāsatvaśaṅkānirākaraṇam antareṇa na śakyate pratipādayitum.*

The prover establishes something that is not known by perception. Without refutation of (legitimate) doubt that this is a pseudo-prover, it would not be able to establish it.

Comments

Inference establishes something that is not cognized through perception (*parokṣa*, "beyond sight"). The fire on the mountain is not perceived; it is, rather, inferred from the smoke which is perceived.

Ratnakīrti's argument is an example of "inference for others," *parārthānumāna*. He is not merely trying to reconstruct a conclusion that he himself knows, but to show it to others who previously did not know it or who even voice the opposite view. Under such circumstances, it is necessary to anticipate legitimate doubts which an opponent might raise as objections to the inference. Sometimes a putative inference is based upon a pseudo-prover (*hetvābhāsa*), which seems to be a good prover, but which does not really entail the conclusion. Ratnakīrti prepares to examine a number of different ways the prover in his inference to momentariness might be defective. In each case, he will show that it is the defects which are not genuine.

Text and Translation (p. 67, line 9)

hetvābhāsāś ca asiddhaviruddhānaikāntikaprabhedena trividhāḥ.

And pseudo-provers are divided into three kinds: the unwarranted, the contradictory, and the inconclusive.

Comments

There are three major kinds of defects that can undermine an inference. A putative prover is said to be "unwarranted" (*asiddha*) when it is not known to qualify the *pakṣa*. For instance, if someone is trying to infer fire on a mountain and cites smoke as the prover but there is no smoke to be seen, then he does not have a justifier (*pramāṇa*) to support the premise that there is smoke there: the prover is unwarranted. The other broad types of defective prover involve problems with the pervasion needed to ground an inference. A putative prover is "contradictory" (*viruddha*) when it occurs only where the probandum does not. This would be exactly the inverse of the pervasion relation needed to ground the inference. Consequently, the inference would prove exactly the opposite of what was intended. For instance, if someone were to purport to infer fire on a mountain using water as prover, that prover would be contradictory, for water only occurs where fire is not. A prover is "inconclusive" (*anaikāntika*, literally "non-uniform") when no universal correlation can be made between it and the probandum. Sometimes the putative prover occurs with the probandum, but sometimes it occurs without it. For instance, to attempt to infer smoke from fire would be to use a prover that is inconclusive, because it is not uniformly correlated with fire. There are cases known where fire occurs without smoke, such as a hot ball of iron (the presence of fire accounting for the heat). The pervasion therefore does not hold and so a purported prover, fire, does not show conclusively that there is smoke.

Text and Translation (p. 67, lines 10–16)

> *tatra na tāvad ayam asiddho hetuḥ. yadi nāma darśane darśane nānāprakāraṃ sattvalakṣaṇam uktam āste, arthakriyākārittvaṃ, sattāsamavāyaḥ, svarūpasattvam, utpādavyayadhrauvyayogitvaṃ, pramāṇaviṣayatvaṃ tadupalambhakapramāṇagocaratvaṃ, vyapadeśaviṣayatvam ityādi, tathāpi kim anenāprastutenedānīm eva niṣṭaṅkitena. yad eva hi pramāṇato nirūpyamāṇaṃ padārthānāṃ sattvam upapannaṃ bhaviṣyati tad eva vayam api svīkariṣyāmaḥ. kevalaṃ tad etad arthakriyākāritvaṃ sarvajanaprasiddham āste tat khalv atra sattvaśabdenābhisandhāya sādhanatvenopāttam.*

Concerning these, first of all, our prover is not unwarranted. It is true that definitions of existence from one system to another are stated whose predicates vary: (a) that which has causal efficiency; (b) that which has existence inhering in it; (c) that which exists by its own nature; (d) that which is suitable to be produced, endure, and be destroyed; (e) that which is an object of the "sources of knowledge," *pramāṇa*; (f) that which is in the field of the *pramāṇa* of perception; (g) that which is the object of words, and others. Nevertheless, what would be the point of working with a definition that is not generally accepted? Now we proceed just with what is impartial. For only that which is determined by *pramāṇa* will be rightly conceived as the existence of things. That alone do we also accept. Only this (definition), causal efficiency, is well-known to everyone. That, indeed, is meant here as the prover for the purpose of agreement with respect to the word "existence."

Comments

An unwarranted prover is a prover which is not known to qualify the *pakṣa*. If Ratnakīrti's prover were unwarranted, then existence would not be known to be found in the cases under dispute. Ratnakīrti seeks to show that the *pakṣa* is qualified by the prover, existence. To this end, he mentions various definitions of existence found in Indian philosophical systems (*darśana*). He rejects all but one of them on the grounds that all but the one is controversial. That one is a minimal definition accepted by all disputants, at least implicitly, namely, the ability to produce a "practical" effect (*arthakriyākāritva*), i.e., an effect that impacts our lives. Ratnakīrti introduces this definition as acceptable to all sides, but, as we shall see, the formulation is also crucial to his argument.

Text and Translation (p. 67, lines 16–18)

tac ca yathāyogaṃ pratyakṣānumānapramāṇaprasiddhasadbhāveṣu bhāveṣu pakṣīkṛteṣu pratyakṣādinā pramāṇena pratītam iti na svarūpeṇāśrayadvāreṇa vāsiddhisaṃbhāvanāpi.

And, therefore, the knowledge sources of perception or inference, as is appropriate, make it known that existence is in these existent things we are taking as the case at issue (*pakṣa*). Therefore, there should not be even a suspicion that it is unwarranted either with respect to itself or to its basis (i.e., that in which it lies, a pot, for instance).

Comments

Everything at issue here exists. That these existent things exhibit existence is known by perception or inference, depending on the type of thing. That the prover qualifies the cases in question is so obvious that we can barely entertain the notion that it does not. Existence cannot be lacking from existent things. The prover is thus not unwarranted (*asiddhi*).

It is also not "unwarranted in its basis" (*āśrayāsiddhi*)—a fallacy that occurs not when the prover is absent from the cases at issue, but when the cases at issue are themselves unreal and thus cannot provide the basis for the presence of the prover. Our prover is not unwarranted in its basis because everything at issue here exists, and a thing is not unreal insofar as it exists. Ratnakīrti's inference and pervasion are *anvaya* in form, between existence and momentariness; the charge of *āśrayāsiddhi* is more serious against the *vyatireka* form, where the pervasion is between non-existence and non-momentariness. There the supporting instances are all non-existent things, which, it can be argued, are simply unreal and cannot form the basis for an inference. Much of the second half of the text is devoted to defending the *vyatireka* form of the inference against this objection.[41]

Text and Translation (p. 67, line 19)

nāpi viruddhatā sapakṣīkṛte ghaṭe sadbhāvāt.

It is also not contradictory, because a pot, which is a similar instance, presents itself as an existent.

Comments

"Similar instance(s)," *sapakṣa*, is a technical term in the theory of inference. Although it is rendered here simply as "similar instance," it is a similar case in a very specific sense. A *sapakṣa* is any case that is claimed to be like the case at issue in being *known* to exhibit the probandum—by the person putting forth the inference and, it is presumed, by the targeted audience as well. This means that if a cited *sapakṣa* is also known to exhibit the prover then it provides a point of positive correlation between the prover and the probandum. For instance, fire is known to exist in a kitchen hearth by A, who is putting forth an inference, and by B, who is A's audience. It is thus a similar instance, *sapakṣa*. And since smoke is also found there, it provides evidence in favor of the pervasion which grounds inference of fire from smoke.

It is worth mentioning at this point that the word *vipakṣa*, which will be rendered as "dissimilar instance(s)," also has a technical meaning. A *vipakṣa* is any case that is claimed to be dissimilar to the case at issue in being known to not exhibit the probandum. If such a case is known to be qualified by the prover, then it provides a counterexample to the pervasion and the entire inference is blocked. If the case is known not to be qualified by the prover, then it provides a point of negative correlation in support of the pervasion. For instance, fire is known not to occur on a lake. A lake is thus a dissimilar case. And if smoke were known to occur there, it would show that the inference of fire from smoke was faulty. Since

[41] See McDermott (1969), pp. 34–50.

we know that smoke does not occur on a lake, citing a lake supports the inference-grounding pervasion between smoke and fire. A good or genuine inference requires at least one similar case to be known to be qualified by the prover, or one dissimilar case to be known not to be qualified by the prover. In Ratnakīrti's inference, a pot is put forth as a similar case because Buddhists regard pots as known examples of momentary things. Since a pot also exists, it provides a point of positive correlation supporting the pervasion between existence and momentariness.

Here Ratnakīrti insists that his prover is not contradictory, because the nature of the things in dispute is not non-existence. If, like a lake, where veritable smoke is never found, the example exhibited an absence of the prover, then there would be a contradictory prover. But here the things under dispute are, like the pot, existent.

Text and Translation (p. 67, lines 19–22)

> *nanu katham asya sapakṣatvam, pakṣavad atrāpi kṣaṇabhaṅgāsiddheḥ. na hy asya pratyakṣataḥ kṣaṇabhaṅgasiddhiḥ, tathātvenāniścayāt. nāpi sattvānumānataḥ, punar nidarśanāntarāpekṣāyām anavasthānaprasaṅgāt. na cānyad anumānam asti. saṃbhave vā tenaiva pakṣe 'pi kṣaṇabhaṅgasiddher alaṃ sattvānumāneneti cet.*

Objection: How can it be a similar instance? Even though it is like the case at issue, momentariness is not established. For its being momentary is not known by perception, because it is not certain that it is like that. It is also not known by inference from existence, because that would entail the unfortunate consequence of infinite regress since there would be needed yet another example. And there is no other inference (that could establish it as momentary). Or, if another inference were possible, then by that alone momentariness would be proved also with respect to the case at issue. So enough with this inference from existence!

Comments

A similar instance is one in which the probandum is known to occur. The existence of the prover in such a case gives us a point of positive correlation in support of the inference-grounding pervasion. In this case, the cited pot is known to exhibit the prover, existence. So if it is a similar case, then it provides evidence for the pervasion between existence and momentariness.

The opponent objects that the pot cannot serve as a similar case because it is not yet established that it exhibits the probandum, momentariness, even though it is like the case in question in exhibiting the prover. The opponent does not accept that the pot is momentary, and argues that the claim that it is momentary cannot be supported by either perception or inference. The pot is perceived, but whether it is momentary or not is not established by perception. Although both disputants perceive the pot, they disagree about whether it endures. Another alternative, the opponent suggests, is that the pot would be established as momentary by the same inference from existence that establishes the momentariness of everything else. The problem is that then we would need another example to support the pervasion between existence and momentariness. This example would also become subject to dispute, and so another inference would be needed and another example. This would lead to an infinite regress (*anavasthā*), and the momentariness of the pot would remain unestablished. If the momentariness of the pot were established by some other inference, then the argument from existence would not be needed and momentariness could be established just by this other inference.

Text and Translation (p. 67, lines 23–24)

> *ucyate. anumānāntaram eva prasaṅgaprasaṅgaviparyayātmakaṃ ghaṭasya kṣaṇabhaṅgaprasādhakaṃ pramāṇāntaram asti.*

Ratnakīrti: We answer. There is indeed another inference. It is a source of knowledge establishing the momentariness of the pot. It has the character of a *prasaṅga* and the transformation of that *prasaṅga*.

Comments

Ratnakīrti admits that the momentariness of the pot has to be established by another argument. This argument takes the form of a *prasaṅga*, which is a refutation based on a bad consequence that follows from some thesis. For instance, if we see smoke on the mountain and you tell me there is no fire there, I can point out that if there were no fire there, there would be no smoke there. In other words, the appropriate response to someone who fails to make the inference or who asks, "But are you sure that there is fire there?" would be to present counterfactual reasoning in support of the inference. This may help the person to see the relationships underpinning the inference. Such counterfactual reasoning would in effect take the form of an indirect proof. Suppose there is no fire there. In that case there would be no smoke. However, we see smoke. Therefore, there is fire.

Now every *prasaṅga* can be transformed into a standard inference whose *vyāpti* takes a contrapositive form. For example, there is fire on the mountain because there is smoke there, and everywhere there is smoke there is fire. Ratnakīrti will now argue that a bad consequence will result if it is assumed that the pot endures for more than a moment. This *prasaṅga* can be transformed into a standard inference distinct from the inference from existence and supporting it.

In sum, there is a two-step argument. (1) Everything that exists is causally efficient, and (2) everything that is causally efficient is momentary. It follows from these two premises that (3) everything that exists is momentary. This is the general rule on which the inference from existence is based. The inference from existence as originally stated hides the fact that these two steps are necessary to make the inference work. In order to support the inference based upon the pervasion stated in (3), Ratnakīrti must show that the example supporting that pervasion is really a case of momentariness. He has already adopted (1) as his definition of existence. So, given that the pot exists and is therefore casually efficient, he can prove that the example is good by using an inference based upon (2). He must of course support the pervasion stated in (2). He does this not by offering another example, which would lead to the infinite regress, but by a refutation based on a bad consequence that would follow if anything that has causal efficiency were to endure. He now presents this *prasaṅga*.

Text and Translation (p. 67, line 24– p. 68, line 2)

> *tathā hi ghaṭo vartamānakṣaṇe tāvad ekām arthakriyāṃ karoti. atītānāgatakṣaṇayor api kiṃ tām evārthakriyāṃ kuryāt, anyāṃ vā, na vā kām api kriyām iti trayaḥ pakṣāḥ.*

To be specific, the pot existing in the present moment produces, first of all, some practical effect. Now would it also cause such a practical effect in past and future moments? Or, would it produce another practical effect? Or, would it not produce any effect at all? These are the three options.

Comments

We know the pot that exists at the present moment produces some practical effect (*arthakriyā*), because by definition anything that exists produces some practical effect. If the pot endures, it must also exist in past and future moments. Ratnakīrti now focuses on what the pot would produce in those past and future moments. He considers three possibilities:

1. The pot produces the same effect in those moments as it does now.

2. The pot produces a different effect than it does now.

3. The pot produces no effect at all.

Ratnakīrti will argue that (1) and (3) are impossible and that (2) implies the pot existing now is a distinct entity from those that exist in the past and the future. This is step one in his project of securing an example for the positive-correlation inference to momentariness.

Text and Translation (p. 68, line 3)

nātra prathamaḥ pakṣo yuktaḥ, kṛtasya karaṇāyogāt.

Of these, the first option is no good because it is inappropriate to speak of making something that has already been made.

Comments

The first option (1) is that the pot produces the same effect in the past and future as it does right now. The problem with this is that if the pot has already produced the effect in the past, it would not need to produce it again in the present. Furthermore, if the pot produces the effect in the present, then there would be no need for it to be produced again in the future. In either case, it is impossible that the pot can produce the same effect in two different moments, because once something is produced it cannot be produced again. Thus it is inappropriate to speak in such a fashion.

Text and Translation (p. 68, lines 4–10)

atha dvitīyo 'bhyupagamyate, tad idam atra vicāryatām. yadā ghaṭo vartamānakṣaṇabhāvi kāryaṃ karoti tadā kim atītānāgatakṣaṇabhāviny api kārye śakto 'śakto vā. yadi śaktas tadā vartamānakṣaṇabhāvikāryavad atītānāgatakṣaṇabhāvy api kāryaṃ tadaiva kuryāt. tatrāpi śaktatvāt. śaktasya ca kṣepāyogāt. anyathā varttamānakṣaṇabhāvino 'pi kāryasyākaraṇaprasaṅgāt. pūrvāparakālayor api śaktatvenāviśeṣāt. samarthasya ca sahakāryapekṣāyā ayogāt. athāśaktaḥ, tadaikatra kārye śaktāśaktatvaviruddhadharmādhyāsāt kṣaṇavidhvaṃso ghaṭasya durvāraprasaraḥ syāt.

Now the second option is accepted (by us). So let us examine it here. Given that the pot existing in the present moment produces an effect, is it able, or unable, to produce with respect to an effect that exists in the past or in the future? If it is able, then, like the effect existing in the present moment, past and future effects would be produced, too, because it would be capable with respect to them, too. There should be no delay on the part of something that has the capability. Otherwise, there would be the unfortunate consequence that the effect is not produced in the present moment. For there would be no difference between an earlier time and a later time in its being able to produce the effect. And it would be improper that there need be an auxiliary cause for something that is capable. Now, (if you assume that it is) not able to produce the effect, then because you would impose incompatible properties, both ability and inability with respect to (production of) a single effect, the conclusion would be irresistible that the pot is destroyed in a moment.

Comments

The second option is that the pot produces a different effect in the past and future moments than it does in the present. This option is accepted by Ratnakīrti on the grounds that if the pot were able to produce the same effect in the past and future then that effect would exist at those moments. It cannot be denied that the effect would exist if the ability to produce it were to occur, because in that case the effect should not exist in the present either. At the other times, the pot would have the same abilities and therefore would produce the same effect.

This only follows, however, if it is assumed that an auxiliary cause (*sahakārin*) is not responsible for the exercising of an unrealized ability. Ratnakīrti rejects this possibility rather casually, but as we will see, it is the most serious objection to his argument.

If the pot is not able to produce the same effect in the past and future, then the pot must be a different entity at each moment. Otherwise, a single entity would be the bearer of incompatible properties (*viruddhadharmādhyāsa*). Ratnakīrti holds that this is the only sensible option. The pot produces a different effect at each instant, and is therefore a distinct entity at each instant.

Text and Translation (p. 68, lines 11–16)

> *nāpi tṛtīyaḥ pakṣaḥ saṅgacchate, śaktasvabhāvānuvṛtter eva. yadā hi śaktasya padārthasya vilambo 'py asahyas tadā dūrotsāritam akaraṇam. anyathā vārtamānikasyāpi kāryasyākaraṇaṃ syād ity uktam. tasmād yad yadā yajjananavyavahārapātraṃ tat tadā tat kuryāt. akurvac ca na jananavyavahārabhājanam. tad evam ekatra kārye samarthetarasvabhāvatayā pratikṣaṇaṃ bhedād ghaṭasya sapakṣatvam akṣatam.*

The third option also does not work because of (the demands of) conformity with the self-nature of something that is able to produce. For since an object that is able to produce would be (on this view) delayed (in producing), it would not be able to produce at that time. (In that case) something produced later would have no cause. Otherwise, there would be no cause of an effect existing in the present, so it has been argued (by us). Therefore, whenever something is properly spoken of as productive of something else, that something at that time would produce (and would be properly spoken of as producing) that something else.

And something not producing something else is not entitled to be spoken of as producing that other thing. Thus, in this way, that a pot is a similar case is not refuted because it is different at every moment according to its self-nature as either capable or incapable of producing an effect at any single moment.

Comments

The third option is that the pot produces no effect in past and future moments. If the pot exists, however, it must be productive; not producing is not consistent with its having a self-nature (*svabhāva*) that is capable of production. It might be argued that it produces no effect even though it is capable of producing because the effect is delayed until the auxiliary factors arrive. However, Ratnakīrti counters, that is not possible because if something does not produce at a given moment it is not worthy of being called capable of producing. Something we designate as capable of producing must produce right then and there. This analysis amounts to the claim that there are no unrealized capacities.

Here Ratnakīrti merely states the claim, but this understanding of "capacity" will continue to be a key point of contention. Later, he will explicitly defend it. Assuming the claim is right, however, Ratnakīrti's supporting proof is complete. Both (1) and (3) are impossible, and therefore (2) is correct and the pot must produce a different effect at each moment. It follows from this that the pot is a distinct entity at each moment. The pot is thus proved to be momentary. It is therefore a similar case, and, since it also exists, it constitutes positive correlation in support of the thesis that pervasion is the relation between existence and momentariness, the prover and probandum of the central inference.

Text and Translation (p. 68, lines 17–18)

> *atra prayogaḥ. yad yadā yajjananavyavahārayogyaṃ tat tadā tajjanayaty eva. yathā antyā kāranasāmagrī svakāryam.*

Here is the formal reconstruction: That *x* at time *y* appropriately spoken of as productive of *z*, that *x* at that time *y* produces *z*, as (on your view) the final, complete collection of causal factors (*sāmagrī*) produces its effect.

Comments

In order to eliminate options (1) and (3), Ratnakīrti has proclaimed that there can be no unrealized capacities. If the pot at a given time is appropriately spoken of as capable of producing some effect, it must actually produce that effect at that time. The argument thus depends on a pervasion between being appropriately spoken of as capable of producing a certain effect and actually producing that effect. Here Ratnakīrti reconstructs the argument formally, citing a positive example to support the pervasion. The example comes from the Nyāya view of causation. A complete collection of causal factors *sufficient* for production of the effect (*sāmagrī* is the Nyāya term)—which is said to come about when a final causal factor, or trigger, arrives—actually produces the effect. This is a supporting example because it is something that all disputants agree is both appropriately spoken of at that time as capable of producing the effect and actually productive of the effect at that time.

Text and Translation (p. 68, lines 19–23)

> *atītānāgatakṣaṇabhāvikāryajananavyavahārayogyaś cāyam ghaṭo vartamānakṣaṇabhāvikāryakaraṇakāle sakalakriyātikramakāle 'pīti svabhāvahetuprasaṅgaḥ. asya ca dvitīyādikṣaṇabhāvikāryakaraṇavyavahāragocaratvasya. prasaṅgasādhanasya vārtamānikakāryakaraṇakāle. sakalakriyātikramakāle ca ghaṭe dharmiṇi parābhyupagamamātrataḥ siddhatvād asiddhis tāvad asaṃbhavinī.*

This pot, which is (according to you) suitable to be spoken of as a cause in a past or future moment, must, at the time it produces the effect that exists at the present time, be productive also at a time after its capacity has been exhausted. This is an unfortunate ramification where the prover is of the "self-nature" type.

The thesis of its being suitable to be spoken of as producing an effect at a second moment, etc., implies an unfortunate consequence that applies to the view that a pot is both productive of the effect at the present moment and after its entire capacity has been exhausted. So just from entertaining your position, it is quite wrong that our proving an untoward ramification suffers from the fault of being unwarranted, because this (suitability for speech) is (according to you) established (in a pot).

Comments

Here Ratnakīrti argues that the untoward ramification he points out is not unwarranted. He has shown that the pot is momentary by showing that the view that it endures leads to an unfortunate consequence. Something worthy of being called productive at a certain time must produce right there and then. The pot would have to produce the same effect both at the present moment and again in the next moment after it had already exhausted its capacity to produce that effect (*sakala-kriyātikrama-kāla*). This cannot be accepted because, as we have seen, it would imply that an effect having already been produced would be produced a second time. It follows from this unfortunate consequence that the pot is momentary. The unfortunate consequence hinges on an essential property, being suitable for speech, etc. The prover in that argument is not unwarranted in the technical sense in that the opponent takes it to apply to a pot. So just from entertaining that position, we find an untoward consequence that hinges on "being suitable to be spoken of as productive."

Text and Translation (p. 68, line 24)

> *nāpi viruddhatā, sapakṣe 'ntyakāraṇasāmagrahyāṃ sadbhāvasaṃbhavāt.*

It is also not contradictory. There is a similar case (according to Nyāya) because of the possibility of its existence when the last causal factor is added completing the total collection (*sāmagrī*) sufficient to produce the effect.

Comments

A prover is contradictory when it is pervaded by the negation of the probandum, the probandum's opposite: everywhere the prover is, the probandum is not. For instance, to use water as the prover in an inference to fire would be contradictory because everywhere there is water there is absence of fire. The prover in the argument for an untoward ramification would be contradictory if nothing could be spoken of as capable of producing. But the Nyāya opponents' "bundle of causal factors," *sāmagrī*, at the moment when the trigger or final causal factor is added such that the collection becomes sufficient to produce the effect, is clearly a similar case, at least in the context of the "untoward ramification" argument, because it is just what the Nyāya opponent speaks of as capable.

Text and Translation (p. 68, lines 25–26)

> *nanv ayaṃ sādhāraṇānaikāntiko hetuḥ. sākṣādajanake 'pi kuśūlādyavasthitabījādau vipakṣe samarthavyavahāragocaratvasya sādhanasya darśanād iti cet.*

Objection: The prover is inconclusive in that it is common to both similar and dissimilar cases. It is seen to be like the seed, etc., situated in the granary, etc., which is a dissimilar case, given that the seed in the granary does not produce immediately, although it is in the scope of being properly talked about as capable.

Comments

A prover is shown to be inconclusive when a counterexample is cited to a professed pervasion between a prover and probandum. For instance, the prover, smoke, would be shown to be inconclusive if there were one case pointed out where there was smoke without fire. Cases known not to exhibit the probandum are, in the technical sense, dissimilar cases (*vipakṣa*). If such a case exhibits the prover, then the prover is inconclusive, *anaikāntika*, literally, "non-uniform"—which is a synonym for another term used by Ratnakīrti and by logicians of all schools, *vyabhicārika*, "deviating," i.e., a prover that deviates from its putative probandum to be found in cases where it is not.

The opponent has already suggested that Ratnakīrti's prover, existence, is inconclusive because it occurs in both similar and dissimilar cases. The seed is, on the opponent's view, a counterexample to Ratnakīrti's proposed pervasion between existence and momentariness, because it is both non-momentary and existent. The opponent now argues that the supporting argument does not help, because it, too, relies on a prover that is inconclusive. The seed does not produce immediately so it is also a dissimilar case in the supporting argument where the prover is being-properly-called-capable and the probandum is producing-immediately. The seed does not produce immediately, so it is a dissimilar case. Yet it can be properly called capable of production.

Text and Translation (p. 68, lines 26–30)

> *na. dvividho hi samarthavyavahāraḥ pāramārthika aupacārikaś ca. tatra yat pāramārthikaṃ jananaprayuktaṃ jananavyavahāragocaratvaṃ tad iha sādhanatvenopāttam. tasya ca kuśūlādyavasthitabījādau kāraṇakāraṇatvād aupacārikajananavyavahāraviṣayabhūte saṃbhavābhāvāt kutaḥ sādhāraṇānaikāntikatā.*

Ratnakīrti: No. For there are two ways of properly talking about capability: the literal and the metaphorical. Of these, to speak properly with respect to production in the literal sense—i.e., to be in the scope of proper talk about production—is what we say here is our prover. Because the seed situated in the granary is a cause of the cause, it can be in the metaphorical sense an object of talk about production. This being so, how is our prover inconclusive and common to both similar and dissimilar cases for the reason that the seed in the granary is not capable, in the literal sense, of being the cause?

Comments

Ratnakīrti now draws a distinction between a metaphorical (*aupacārika*) and a literal (*pāramārthika*) sense of "capable." In the literal sense, something is capable only if it is able to produce without outside assistance. Ratnakīrti thinks that this is the primary meaning of "capable," applicable when we are speaking strictly of what exists. He makes clear that this is the sense he has in mind when he makes his inference. The seed in the granary, however, is not capable of producing the sprout without outside help, and so it cannot serve as a counterexample. It is capable of producing the sprout in the metaphorical sense, because it produces the next seed-moment in the series in which eventually the capable seed arises. In this way, the metaphorical sense in which something can be said to be capable to produce a future effect through a series of intermediate steps derives from the literal sense in which things are properly said to be capable only if they produce immediately.

Text and Translation (p. 69, lines 1–4)

> *na cāsya sandigdhavyatirekitā, viparyaye bādhakapramāṇasadbhāvāt. tathā hīdaṃ jananavyavahāragocaratvaṃ niyataviṣayatvena vyāptam iti sarvajanānubhavaprasiddham. na cedaṃ nirnimittam deśakālasvabhāvaniyamābhāvaprasaṅgāt. na ca jananād anyan nimittam upalabhyate, tadanvayavyatirekānuvidhānadarśanāt.*

This is not an inference in which the negative form of the pervasion is doubtful, because of the existence of a *pramāṇa* that blocks doubt with respect to the transposed form of the pervasion. For example, those things in the scope of being-properly-talked-about-as-producing are pervaded by being-an-object-restricted (to those things that are currently producing). This is established by the experience of all people. And it is not the case that this is without reason, because otherwise there would be the unfortunate consequence that there would be no restriction with respect to place, time, and self-nature. And a reason other than the fact that it is producing is not found, because we see both positive and negative correlations (between being-properly-spoken-about-as-productive and being-immediately-productive).

Comments

We are concerned here with the supporting inference grounded by a pervasion between (a) being-properly-spoken-about-as-productive and (b) being-immediately-productive. We have seen that this pervasion is supported by examples of positive correlation (*anvaya*), such as the sufficient collection (*sāmagrī*) that both produces immediately and is properly spoken of as productive. The pervasion should also be supported by examples of negative correlation (*vyatireka*), i.e., causes that do not produce immediately and are not properly spoken of as producing. Ratnakīrti is anticipating the objection that the negative correlation is doubtful because there are no available examples from the Buddhist point of view. We know that Ratnakīrti holds that there is no delayed production. This excludes the possibility of dissimilar cases (*vipakṣa*), which would be potential examples of negative correlation.

In the passage at hand, Ratnakīrti argues that a *pramāṇa*, a "knowledge source," blocks doubt concerning the negative correlation. First, there is the positive correlation itself, which has already been established by positive examples and which (as Ratnakīrti himself will argue later on) is equivalent to the negative correlation by the law of transposition. There is also a bad consequence that follows if the negative correlation is denied. If it is not the case that things that do not produce immediately are not properly talked about as productive, then it follows that things whose production is delayed can be properly talked about as productive. This would mean that anything anywhere could be said to be productive of anything else no matter how far in the future or how distant in space the effect were to occur. However, we only properly speak of something as a producer if it is actually producing here and now. Finally, Ratnakīrti points out, the negative correlation is indeed supported by examples. There are many things that both Buddhists and Naiyāyikas agree are not within the scope of proper talk of production with respect to a given effect, and none of these is an immediate producer of that effect. For instance, a stone is not properly talked about as a producer of a sprout and it is also not an immediate producer of a sprout. It thus serves as confirmation of the negative form of the pervasion. Anything that was alleged to be a delayed producer, like the seed in the granary, would be part of the subject at issue in the inference and thus not available as a counterexample.

Text and Translation (p. 69, lines 5–10)

> *yadi ca jananam antareṇāpi jananavyavahāragocaratvaṃ syāt tadā sarvasya sarvatra jananavyavahāre ity aniyamaḥ syāt. niyataś cāyaṃ pratītaḥ. tato jananābhāve vipakṣe niyataviṣayatvasya vyāpakasya nivṛttau nivartamānaṃ jananavyavahāragocaratvaṃ janana eva viśrāmyatīti vyāptisiddher anavadyo hetuḥ. na caiṣa ghaṭo varttamānakāryakaraṇakṣaṇe sakalakriyātikramaṇe cātītānāgatakṣaṇabhāvi kāryaṃ janayati. tato na jananavyavahārayogyaḥ, sarvaḥ prasaṅgaḥ prasaṅgaviparyayaniṣṭha iti nyāyāt.*

And if something were appropriately spoken of as producing even without producing, then there would be no restriction with respect to proper talk of productiveness for anything anywhere. But it is known that there is restriction (with respect to proper talk about producing). Therefore, concerning dissimilar cases, which are cases of the absence of production, there is no being an object restricted (to those things that are currently producing). Such does not fall within the scope of talk of producing. And so, with respect to producing, the cases are excluded, and thus there is a pervasion that establishes that our prover is not objectionable.

And it is not the case that this (pot) produces a past or future effect either at the present time or at a time beyond that when its causal power is exhausted. Therefore it is not suitable for appropriate talk of producing, because of the principle that every unfortunate consequence is related to an inference based on the transformation of that unfortunate consequence.

Comments

Ratnakīrti points out that our speech is restricted with respect to what counts as "productive." There is thus a bad consequence if we deny the negative correlation (everything not producing is not appropriately spoken of as productive). Dissimilar cases (*vipakṣa*) here are those where there is no producing, which means there is no current production. Given this restriction on when it is appropriate to talk of something as productive, such cases must not be within the scope of such talk. A negative correlation is thus established between not currently producing and not being in the scope of proper talk of production. It is established by taking a refutation following on a bad consequence (in this case that there would be no restriction regarding production talk) and transforming it into an inference based on negative correlations (with a transposed *vyāpti*), a pervasion in this case between not currently producing and not being worthy of being talked about as producing. Since Ratnakīrti has already shown that the pot cannot produce the same effect at two different times, it follows that the pot at the later time is not worthy of being called productive of the previous effect.

Text and Translation (p. 69, lines 11–14)

> *atrāpi prayogaḥ. yad yadā yan na karoti na tat tadā tatra samarthavyavahārayogyam. yathā śālyaṅkuram akurvan kodravaḥ śālyaṅkure. na karoti caiṣa ghaṭo vartamānakṣaṇabhāvikāryakaraṇakāle. sakalakriyātikramakāle cātītānāgatakṣaṇabhāvi kāryam iti vyāpakānupalabdhir bhinatti samarthakṣaṇād asamarthakṣaṇam.*

Here also is the formal reconstruction. That x which at time y does not produce z, that x at that time y is not suitable to be properly spoken of as capable of producing with respect to z. Just as barley, which does not produce a rice sprout, is not spoken of as the cause of a rice sprout. And neither at the time when it produces the effect in the present moment nor at a time when its entire capacity is exhausted does a pot produce an effect that exists in a past or future moment. Therefore, the non-cognition of the pervader (i.e., not being fit to be spoken of as producing) distinguishes the incapable moment from the capable.

Comments

Ratnakīrti presents the formal reconstruction of the inference based on the negative correlation between not actually producing a certain effect at a certain time and not being properly spoken of as producing that effect at that time. The supporting example for the pervasion is a barley seed which does not produce a rice sprout and is also not spoken of as capable of producing a rice sprout. The rice seed's capacity to produce a rice sprout is at issue when the seed is in the granary, and cannot be cited as evidence for or against the pervasion in its negative form. The barley seed, however, is acceptable because both sides agree that it is not capable of producing the rice sprout and that it is not properly spoken of as capable of producing the rice sprout, i.e., that it exhibits the absence both of the probandum and the prover. The issue here is whether the pot can serve as a supporting example for the momentariness inference from existence. The inference now in focus supports the premise that the pot is momentary, since it does not produce future effects in the current moment and cannot, therefore, be said to have the capacity to produce those effects. Once it has exhausted its current capacity, it also cannot be said to be capable of producing that effect. The pot is thus distinct at each moment because it cannot be said to have the same capacity in any other moment. It follows that the pot is a similar case (*sapakṣa*) and can serve as a supporting example in the inference from existence on the basis of positive correlation, which is our main concern.

Text and Translation (p. 69, lines 15–19)

> *atrāpy asiddhir nāsti, vartamānakṣaṇabhāvikāryakaraṇakāle sakalakriyātikramakāle cātītānāgatakṣaṇabhāvikāryakaraṇasyāyogāt. nāpi virodhaḥ, sapakṣe bhāvāt. na cānaikāntikatā, pūrvoktena nyāyena samartha-vyavahāragocaratvajanakatvayor vidhibhūtayoḥ sarvopasaṃhāravatyā vyāpteḥ prasādhanāt.*

This formal reconstruction is also not subject to the fallacy of its prover being unwarranted. For it is not right that there is production of past and future effects existing either at the time of the production of the effect that exists at the present moment or at a time after its capacity is exhausted.

It also is not subject to a charge of contradictoriness because there is a similar case.

And it is not inconclusive due to the previously stated argument, because we have proved an all-inclusive pervasion between being-in-the-scope-of-proper-speech-about-capable-things and being-a-producer, which is the positive form of the pervasion.

Comments

Ratnakīrti now shows that his reconstruction is not fallacious, having a prover subject to a charge of being unwarranted, inconclusive, or contradictory. If the fallacy of being unwarranted were committed, it would not be known that the prover, non-production, qualifies the case at issue, the *pakṣa*, which is the pot. The pot, however, is known to be non-productive of its future and past effects both at the current moment and at moments after its effects have been produced. Ratnakīrti has already shown this with his previous argument.

In order to show that the prover is non-contradictory, all that is needed is a single case that displays both it and the probandum. The example of the barley seed shows that it is possible that non-production and not-being-properly-spoken-of-as-producing can occur together.

Finally, it would be wrong to charge inconclusiveness because we have many examples of non-producers which are not spoken of as producing. There are no counterexamples because anything that one might cite as a counterexample is at issue in the inference. For instance, the rice seed is at issue with respect to whether, when it is not producing, it is proper to speak of it as productive of a rice sprout. Thus the pervasion, stated here in its positive form, is established through negative correlation as well as positive correlation, and therefore, given that the pot exhibits the prover, the inference is sound.

Text and Translation (p. 69, lines 20–22)

> *yat punar atroktam, yad yadā yan na karoti na tad tadā tatra samartham ity atra kaḥ karotyarthaḥ. kiṃ kāraṇatvam. uta kāryotpādānuguṇasahakārisākalyam. ahosvit kāryāvyabhicāraḥ. kāryasaṃbandho veti.*

Objection: What is the meaning of "produces" in this case where you say, "That *x* which at time *y* does not produce *z*, that *x* at that time *y* is not suitable to be properly spoken of as capable of producing with respect to *z*?" Is it (1) "to be a cause," (2) "the entirety of the auxiliary factors conducive to production of the effect," (3) "non-deviation from the effect," or (4) "connection to the effect?"

Comments

The opponent now asks what the word "produces" (*karoti*) means in the formal reconstruction of the negative form of the inference for immediate production. The opponent offers four possibilities:

1. Being a cause (*kāraṇatva*)

2. The entire collection of auxiliary factors (*sahakārī-sākalyam*)

3. Non-deviation from the effect (*kāryāvyabhicāra*)

4. Connection to the effect (*kārya-saṃbandha*)

Ratnakīrti now proceeds to reject all but the first option, maintaining that to produce something is to be its cause.

Text and Translation (p. 69, lines 22–27)

> *tatra kāraṇatvam eva karotyarthaḥ. tataḥ pakṣāntarabhāvino dośā anabhyupagamapratihatāḥ. na cātra pakṣe kāraṇatvasāmarthyayoḥ paryāyatvena vyāpakānupalambhasya sādhyāviśiṣṭatvam abhidhātum ucitam, samarthavyavahāragocaratvābhāvasya sādhyatvāt. kāraṇatvasamarthavyavahāragocaratvayoś ca vṛkṣaśiṃśapayor iva vyāvṛttibhedo 'stīty anavasara evaivaṃvidhasya kṣudrapralāpasya.*

Ratnakīrti: Of these four, "causality" is the meaning of "produces." Therefore, faults existing on the other alternatives are blocked by our non-acceptance of them.

Furthermore, it is not right to allege that because "causality" (*kāraṇatva*) and "capacity" (*samārtha*) are synonyms, there is, given non-cognition of the pervader (i.e., causality), non-qualification by the probandum (i.e., produces), because the probandum is absence of being within the scope of proper talk of being capable. These two, "causation" and "capacity" (*samārtha*), are, in the scope of speech, like "tree" and "*śiṃśapa*" (which is a kind of tree). There is a difference in what they exclude. Thus there is no occasion for this idle chatter.

Comments

Ratnakīrti rejects the other three alternatives and accepts "causality" (*kāraṇatva*) as the meaning of "produces" (*karoti*). The problems faced by those other definitions are thus irrelevant.

Next he considers a problem faced by his own definition. If "causality" and "capacity" are synonyms, then the prover, non-production, is identical to the probandum. From this, the probandum, not-being-properly-talked-about-as-capable, is inferred. When the pot is not producing, it must be a non-cause, because by definition production is just causality. If "causality" (*kāraṇatva*) is also synonymous with "capacity" (*samārtha*), then the pot would already be known to possess the probandum as well. And so there would be no need for inference. This is a commonly cited epistemic flaw. Ratnakīrti's response is to claim that the two words are not synonymous. Capacity is a type of causality, just as a *śiṃśapa* is a type of tree. The class of things excluded by the word "causality" is different from the class of things excluded by the word "capacity." There is thus no basis for a complaint that the prover is identical to the probandum.

Text and Translation (p. 69, lines 28–31)

> *tad evaṃ prasaṅgaprasaṅgaviparyayahetudvayabalato ghaṭe dṛṣṭānte kṣaṇabhaṅgaḥ siddhaḥ. tat kathaṃ sattvād anyad anumānaṃ dṛṣṭānte kṣaṇabhaṅgasādhakaṃ nāstīty ucyate. na caivaṃ sattvahetor vaiyarthyam, dṛṣṭāntamātra eva prasaṅgaprasaṅgaviparyayābhyāṃ kṣaṇabhaṅgaprasādhanāt.*

Therefore, in this way, momentariness is proved with respect to the example of the pot through the force of two provers (in two inferences), a *prasaṅga* and its transformation. How, then, can it be said that there is no inference, other than that from existence, to establish momentariness with respect to the example? Yet this inference, whose ground is existence, is not useless, because there is proof of destruction in a moment with respect to just this example in focus (the pot) by means of the two inferences, a *prasaṅga* and its transformation.

Comments

Our momentariness inference from existence is supported by the example of the pot. The pot exhibits the prover, existence, and since it also exhibits the probandum, momentariness, it provides positive evidence in support of the universal thesis of pervasion between existence and momentariness. The argument in support of taking the pot to be such a genuine example proves that it is momentary through two subordinate inferences.

The pot is momentary because it does not produce past or future effects in the present. Anything that produces a different effect is a different entity. This pot is not a different entity. The prover here is not-producing-past-or-future-effects and the probandum is being-an-entity-distinct-from-something-producing-past-or-future-effects. This inference is a transformation of the following *prasaṅga*: if the pot were non-momentary, it would produce future effects right now.

The counterfactual premise is supported by a second argument that we have seen and may also be intended by Ratnakīrti here, though it is probably the one just sketched that he means with the phrase "a *prasaṅga* and its transformation": the pot must produce all the effects of which it is capable immediately, because it is properly spoken of as capable. Anything properly spoken of as capable of producing something, produces it immediately. Now this is also based upon a *prasaṅga*, a counterfactual premise and drawing out of an untoward consequence of a wrong view: if the pot were not to produce immediately, it would not be worthy of being spoken of as capable. Of course, it is spoken of as capable. The prover in the second inference is being-properly-talked-about-as-capable and the probandum is producing. The pervasion is supported both by positive examples, e.g., a complete collection of causal factors, and negative examples, e.g., a barley seed, which does not produce a rice sprout and is not properly said to be capable of doing so.

Ratnakīrti's point is that such supporting inferences are not intended, by themselves, to prove that everything is momentary. Rather, they secure what might otherwise be considered a controversial example as genuine. The supporting reasoning is thus no substitute for the inference from existence itself. That inference is not useless; it accomplishes the task of proving that everything that exists is momentary. The example we give for that inference is indeed supported by subordinate inferences involving *prasaṅga*. The argument from existence is nevertheless useful as the main argument, because it makes it clear that the proof applies to everything that exists, as Ratnakīrti now explains.

Text and Translation (p. 70, lines 1–6)

> *nanv ābhyām eva pakṣe 'pi kṣaṇabhaṅgasiddhir astv iti cet. astu, ko doṣaḥ. yo hi pratipattā prativastu yad yadā yajjananavyavahārayogyaṃ tat tadā taj janayati ityādikam upanyasitum analasas tasya tata eva kṣaṇabhaṅgasiddhiḥ. yas tu prativastu tannnyāyopanyāsaprayāsabhīruḥ sa khalv ekatra dharmiṇi yad yadā yajjananavyavahārayogyaṃ tat tadā taj*

janayati ityādinyāyena sattvamātram astairyavyāptam avadhārya sattvād evānyatra kṣaṇikatvam avagacchatīti, katham apramatto vaiyartham asyācakṣīta.

Objection: Okay, let us accept that there is proof of destruction in a moment by just these two only with respect to the case at issue.

Ratnakīrti: Let us accept it indeed. What fault is there? For, a person who is quick to adduce with respect to everything that it falls under the principle that begins "That *x* which at time *y* is suitable to be spoken of as producing *z*, that *x* at that time *y* produces *z*" has momentariness proved for him. However, a person who is afraid to try to adduce by that method that everything is momentary, such a person understands only with respect to a single property-bearer that it falls under the principle that begins "That *x* which at time *y* is suitable to be spoken of as producing *z*, that *x* at that time *y* produces *z*." Having determined that existence itself is pervaded by impermanence, one knows momentariness by means of (knowing) existence. How could an attentive person say that this is useless?

Comments

Even if the supporting argument were to be taken as an alternative inference for universal momentariness, there would be no fault. Indeed, the inference could have been constructed to show that momentariness follows for all causally efficient things directly from their causal efficiency. Some might immediately see that this applies to everything that exists. Ratnakīrti does not, however, use that strategy. He only uses the supporting inference to establish the momentariness of the pot as a supporting example for the inference from existence, because it may not be obvious to everyone that the momentariness of everything follows directly from everything's having causal efficiency. The argument is thus given in several steps, where the argument from existence is the main inference and the others play a supporting role. The main inference is not useless because it makes it clear that the argument proves the momentariness of everything existing.

Text and Translation (p. 70, lines 6–10)

tad evam ekakāryakāriṇo ghaṭasya dvitīyādikṣaṇabhāvikāryāpekṣayā samarthetarasvabhāvaviruddhadharmādhyāsād bheda eveti

> *kṣaṇabhaṅgitayā sapakṣatām āvahati ghaṭe sattvahetur upalabhyamāno na viruddhaḥ. na cāyam anaikāntikaḥ, atraiva sādharmyavati dṛṣṭānte sarvopasaṃhāravatyā vyāpteḥ prasādhanāt.*

In this way, because there is upon the pot, which produces a single effect, superimposition of the contrary properties being-capable and not-being-capable with respect to an effect that is to exist in a second and so on moment, it is distinct (from the pot in the second and so on moments). Therefore, our prover, existence—being experienced with respect to the pot, which bears the burden of the similar case because it is momentary—is not contradictory (with the probandum).

And it is not inconclusive, because, given that the example is in this case similar, the proof of the pervasion is by the route of including everything.

Comments

Ratnakīrti spells out the other steps in the argument. Superimposition explains the tendency of the opponent to take a pot, etc., to endure. The pot is not really capable of producing future effects, but it is thought to be so in being imagined to endure. It really produces its effect only at the present moment, and so it is really distinct from the entities that produce those future effects. In this way, it is shown that the pot is momentary. The pot thus qualifies as a similar case in the inference from existence, and so the prover of that inference, existence, is not contradictory. It is also not inconclusive because the pervasion between existence and momentariness is extrapolated from the example of the pot, which has been shown to be qualified by both the prover and the probandum, with no known counterexamples.

Text and Translation (p. 70, lines 10–16)

> *nanu viparyayabādhakapramāṇabalād vyāptisiddhiḥ. tasya copanyāsavārtāpi nāsti. tat kathaṃ vyāptiḥ prasādhiteti cet. tad etat taralabuddhivilasitam. tathā hi uktam etad vartamānakṣaṇabhāvikāryakaraṇakāle 'tītānāgata-kṣaṇabhāvikārye 'pi ghaṭasya śaktisaṃbhave tadānīm eva tatkaraṇam. akaraṇe ca śaktāśaktasvabhāvatayā pratikṣaṇaṃ bheda iti kṣaṇikatvena vyāptaiva sā arthakriyāśaktiḥ. nanv evam*

anvayamātram astu. vipakṣāt punar ekāntena vyāvṛttir iti kuto labhyata iti cet. vyāptisiddher eva. vyatirekasandehe vyāptisiddhir eva katham iti cet.

Objection: The pervasion (grounding your inference) is (you say) established by the power of a knowledge source (*pramāṇa*) that blocks the opposite conclusion. And (yet) there is no occasion at all for the employment of such a knowledge source (since momentariness is everywhere evident). How, then, is the pervasion to become well-known?

Ratnakīrti: It comes to be manifest (gradually) to us who are of inconstant minds. For example, it has been argued that if a pot has the power to produce past and future effects, too, then it should produce them right now, at the present time when it is producing the present effect (having the power now). If it can have that power, then right then it should bring them about. And if it is not bringing them about, then it is different at every moment due to its nature being (at one time) able and (at another time) unable. Power to produce a practical effect is pervaded by momentariness.

Objection: Let this inference based only on positive considerations stand (for the sake of argument). Since, however, the prover is absolutely excluded from dissimilar cases (of which there are none), how would it (a negative pervasion) be grasped?

Ratnakīrti: Just through the establishing of the pervasion (between having the power to produce and momentariness).

Objection: How can it be just the establishment of the pervasion if there is doubt about negative correlations (as indeed there is, since it cannot be ruled out)?

Comments

The pervasion between having the capacity to produce and momentariness is, according to Ratnakīrti established by a *pramāṇa* that defeats the opposite supposition. A pot can produce an effect only at one moment, and this defeats the possibility that a producer can exist at more than one time. The opponent grants for the sake of argument that the pervasion can be established by positive correlations, but argues that there remains doubt about the support from negative correlations. Negative correlations seem impossible to find because all candidates are disputed. Dissimilar cases are those not qualified by the probandum, momentariness, namely, things that are non-momentary. However, on the Buddhist view there are no non-momentary things, so no dissimilar cases are available. This means that there are no examples supporting the negative correlation and doubt thus remains about the pervasion.

Text and Translation (p. 70, lines 17–28)

> *na. dvividhā hi vyāptisiddhiḥ. anvaya-rūpā ca kartṛdharmaḥ sādhanadharmavati dharmiṇi sādhyadharmasyāvaśyambhāvo yaḥ, vyatirekarūpā ca karmadharmaḥ sādhyābhāve sādhanasyāvaśyambhāvo yaḥ. enayoś caikatarapratītir niyamena dvitīyapratītim ākṣipati. anyathaikasyā evāsiddheḥ. tasmād yathā viparyaye bādhakapramāṇabalāt niyamavati vyatireke siddhe 'nvayaviṣayaḥ saṃśayaḥ pūrvaṃ sthito 'pi paścāt parigalati tato 'nvayaprasādhanārthaṃ na pṛthak sādhanam ucyate tathā prasaṅgatadviparyayahetudvayabalato niyamavaty anvaye siddhe vyatirekaviṣaye pūrvaṃ sthito 'pi sandehaḥ paścāt parigalaty eva. na ca vyatirekaprasādhakam anyat pramāṇaṃ vaktavyam. tataś ca sādhyābhāve sādhanasyaikāntiko vyatirekaḥ. sādhane sati sādhyasyāvaśyam anvayo veti na kaścid arthabhedaḥ. tad evaṃ viparyaya-bādhakapramāṇam antareṇāpi prasaṅgaprasaṅgaviparyaya-hetudvayabalād anvayarūpavyāptisiddhau sattvahetor anaikāntikatvasyābhāvād ataḥ sādhanāt kṣaṇabhaṅgasiddhir anavadyeti.*

Ratnakīrti: No. For the pervasion is established in two ways: the positive form (*anvaya*), which is a necessary relation of the probandum property to anything that exhibits the prover property; and the negative form (*vyatireka*), which is the necessity of the prover quality being absent where the probandum is absent. Each one of these two implies and follows by rule from the other. Otherwise, neither could be established.

Given that negative correlation has been established by rule, even though a doubt about positive correlation occurs at first, it disappears afterwards from the force of a *pramāṇa* that blocks the opposite. Therefore it is said "that whose purpose is to establish positive correlation is not a separate demonstration." In this way, given that rule-bound positive correlation, which includes in its range negative correlation, has been established, by the force of a pair of provers, a *prasaṅga* and its transformation, doubt that previously has arisen simply disappears afterwards.

And it is not the case that another *pramāṇa* that proves the negative correlation is to be identified. And therefore where the probandum is absent the prover is correspondingly absent absolutely (if the pervasion has been established by positive means). Or, given the presence of the prover, the co-presence (*anvaya*) of the probandum is necessary. Therefore, there is no difference in meaning.

Therefore, in this way, even without a *pramāṇa* that blocks the opposite (with respect to the negative correlation), there is proof of a pervasion by means of positive correlation through the power of two provers, each a *prasaṅga* and its transformation. Because there is no inconclusiveness with respect to the prover, existence, our proof of momentariness is unobjectionable.

Comments

Ratnakīrti argues that there are positive (*anvaya*) and negative (*vyatireka*) rules that express a single pervasion and that are thus logically equivalent. In other words, here he defends the law of transposition:

$$(\phi \rightarrow \varphi) \equiv (\sim\varphi \rightarrow \sim\phi).$$

So, even though there is no distinct *pramāṇa* to show negative correlation (absence of causal efficiency in non-momentary things), the relevant inference-grounding pervasion is established nonetheless. Positive correlation (presence of momentariness in anything that is causally efficient) is established by the inferences obtained through the *prasaṅgas* and their transformation into inferences with a transposed *vyāpti*. Therefore, if doubt about negative correlation arises, it is put to rest by the inference based on positive correlation. Pervasion can be entirely established by either positive or negative correlation alone, because the positive and negative forms of the inference-grounding rule are logically equivalent.

Text and Translation (p. 71, lines 1–5)

nanu ca sādhanam idam asiddham. na hi kāraṇabuddhyā kāryaṃ gṛhyate, tasya bhāvitvāt. na ca kāryabuddhyā kāraṇam, tasyātītatvāt. na ca vartamānagrāhiṇā jñānenātītānāgatayor grahaṇam, atiprasaṅgāt. na ca pūrvāparayoḥ kālayor ekaḥ pratisandhātā asti, kṣaṇabhaṅgabhaṅgaprasaṅgāt. kāraṇābhāve tu kāryābhāvapratītiḥ svasaṃvedanavādino manorathasyāpy aviṣayaḥ.

Objection (by objector 1, Bhāsarvajña): Your prover is unwarranted (asiddha, i.e., not shown to qualifiy the pakṣa). For, it is not the case that an effect is grasped through a cognition of its cause, since it is (still) to be. And a cause is not grasped through a cognition of its effect, since it is past. And there is no grasping of the past and future through a cognition grasping what exists in the present, because of impossible application. And (on your view) there is not a single recollector of both a past and a future time, because (otherwise) there is the bad consequence of the collapse of (your view that there is) destruction in a moment. Even though you desire there to be cognition of the absence of the effect in the absence of the cause, this is not, however, a coherent view for one who holds that consciousness (including "grasping") is self-illuminating.

Comments

The opponent, whom we may presume to be or to echo the Naiyāyika Bhāsarvajña (see below, *Text and Translation* p. 72, line 10, where his *Nyāyabhūṣaṇa* is mentioned), charges that the Buddhist view makes it impossible to grasp a pot as causally efficient. This would render the prover "unwarranted" in the technical sense of not being shown to qualify the *pakṣa*, the inferential subject. In other words, causal efficiency would not be known to qualify the pot. A cause has to be in the past, whereas an effect is in the present. One and the same cognition cannot grasp both. In the Nyāya view, in order to form a cognition of a causal relation, there must be a cognizer with access to the cognition of both cause and effect. This would be possible only if there were an enduring cognizer who, having experienced the cause, could remember it later, at the time of cognition of the effect. Only in this way could a cognition relating the two be formed (see e.g., *Nyāya-sūtra-bhāṣya* 3.1.1). The Buddhists, however, deny any single enduring entity that could experience both (*pratisandhātṛ*).

Ratnakīrti's argument requires recourse to the idea of causal relations because it depends crucially upon things such as the example of the pot being known as causes. But he has no right to this concept, the opponent charges, because no entity has access to both a cognition of something in the present and a cognition of something as past.

Since Buddhists, furthermore, insist that cognitions are self-illumining (*svasaṃvedana*), there cannot be a delay in a cognition's making its object known. One cognition does not reveal another cognition; rather each cognition reveals itself along with its object. Cognitions are differentiated according to their objects, and at every moment both cognition and object are changing. There would be thus no way, the Naiyāyika charges, to form a cognition of a connection between a cause and an effect.

Text and Translation (p. 71, lines 5–10)

> *nanu ca pūrvottarakālayoḥ saṃvittī, tābhyāṃ vāsanā, tayā ca hetuphalāvasāyo vikalpa iti cet tad ayuktam. sa hi vikalpo gṛhītānusandhāyako 'tadrūpasamāropako vā. na prathamaḥ pakṣaḥ. ekasya pratisandhātur abhāve pūrvāparagrahaṇayor ayogāt vikalpavāsanāyā evābhāvāt. nāpi dvitīyaḥ. marīcikāyām api jalavijñānasya prāmāṇyaprasaṅgāt. tad evam anvayavyatirekayor apratipatter arthakriyālakṣaṇam sattvam asiddham iti.*

Objection (by objector 2 to objector 1): There is a collective self-cognition of the previous and the later (moments). From these two, a memory disposition (*vāsanā*) is produced (containing information from both), and by means of a conceptual construction (*vikalpa*) that is a determination of the cause and effect.

Response (by objector 1, Bhāsarvajña): This is not right. For there is the following dilemma: either your so-called "conceptual construction" (*vikalpa*) amounts to a transtemporal connection (*anusandhāyaka*, a connection between the cognition of the cause and the cognition of the effect) being grasped or it amounts to a superimposition of something false.

It is not the first option, because there simply is no memory impression of your idea. Since there is no single re-cognizer (with access to both cognitions), there is no connection between the earlier and later graspings.

It is also not the second option. For this lands you in the unfortunate consequence that a cognition of water will be veridical even if it is a mirage. Therefore, in this way, because there is no observation of negative and positive correlation, (your prover) existence, defined as causal efficiency, is unwarranted, *asiddha* (in that causal efficiency, being incompatible with momentariness, cannot be shown to qualify the case in question).

Comments

The Nyāya opponent, Bhāsarvajña, anticipates the standard Buddhist response to his objection of the previous passage. This is voiced by objector 2. The notion of a causal relation is formed in the same way that pervasions are known. Two cognitions inform a collective self-cognition (*saṃvittī*), which allows a person to become aware of a cause as preceding its effect. This cognition then forms a memory impression (*vāsanā*), which in turn can become the basis for knowledge of causal relations in general.

Bhāsarvajña or his stand-in rejects this account, reasoning that neither a collective self-cognition nor the availability of memory makes sense on the Buddhist view. There cannot be any collective self-cognition informed by cognitions of both cause and effect, because the two occur at different times, and therefore belong to different cognizers, according to the Buddhist. No collective cognition can be the result of memory, nor can a memory impression give rise to awareness of pervasion, because, again, the rememberer would be distinct from the original cognizer of the remembered object.

The other alternative in the dilemma alleged here is to argue that any idea of a causal relation would be merely made up, or superimposed, by a cognizer of an effect with no basis in any earlier experience of its cause. The problem with this maneuver is that it implies that illusions like the mirage are real. The Buddhist definition of existence (*sattva*) is causal efficiency. If causal relations are now illusory, how can causal efficiency be the mark of the real, the genuinely existent (*sat*)? If the Buddhist insists that it is, then even the mirage of the oasis in the desert should have the capacity to quench thirst.

Text and Translation (p. 71, lines 11–16)

> *kiṃ ca prakārāntarād apīdaṃ sādhanam asiddham. tathā hi bījādīnāṃ sāmarthyaṃ bījādijnānāt tatkāryād aṅkurāder vā niścetavyam. kāryatvaṃ ca vastutvasiddhau sidhyati. vastutvaṃ ca kāryāntarāt. kāryāntarasyāpi kāryatvaṃ vastutvasiddhau. tadvastutvaṃ ca tadaparakāryāntarād ity anavasthā. athānavasthābhayāt paryante kāryāntaraṃ nāpekṣate, tadā tenaiva pūrveṣām asattvaprasaṅgān naikasyāpy arthasāmarthyaṃ sidhyati.*

(Objector 1 continues:) Moreover, this prover is unwarranted in another way. That seeds etc. have capacity is ascertained either from cognition of the seed etc. or from (an inference from sight of) the sprout etc. as its effect. And this effecthood is known on the condition of its being known as a real thing, and its being a real thing is known by its producing another effect. The effecthood of this other effect is, moreover, known on the condition of its being known as real. And its reality is known because it produces yet another effect, different from itself. Thus there is an infinite regress.

Objection (by objector 2): In the end, one effect does not depend upon another (to be known), on pain of infinite regress.

Objector 1: For the very reason you cite, causal efficiency is not shown for any one of them (in your series of effects), because of the unfortunate consequence that (according to your criterion) the previous ones do not exist.

Comments

Our Bhāsarvajña, the Naiyāyika objector 1, offers a second argument to show that causal efficiency is not known to qualify the pot: on Buddhist assumptions, such knowledge would lead to an infinite regress. That something has capacity is known either directly from the cognition of the entity, insofar as it is capable of producing that cognition, or it is known from observation of some other effect it produces. The seed is known to have capacity either directly from our observation of it or from observation of the sprout it produces. In either case, however, the effect also needs to be shown to be real (sometimes our cognition is non-veridical), and this requires that it too be known to produce an effect. In order to show that effect to be real, yet another effect would be required and so on infinitely. Consequently, it cannot be established that the case in question exhibits casual efficiency.

The Buddhist cannot answer that the pot is known to be causally efficient because it produces an effect while the effect it produces does not need to be known as real, i.e., to produce another effect, because in that case it is admitted that the effect is not known as real. If the effect is not known to be real, there remains doubt about the causal efficiency of the pot. If its effect is not real, it is not genuinely causally efficient. Consequently, the prover is unwarranted, since it is not known to qualify the pot at issue.

Text and Translation (p. 71, lines 17–18)

nanu kāryatvasattvayor bhinnavyāvṛttikatvāt sattāsiddhāv api kāryatvasiddhau kā kṣatir iti cet.

Objection (by objector 2 to objector 1): There is a difference in the exclusions of "effecthood" and "existence" (the terms apply to different sets of particulars). If effecthood is shown even when existence is not, what harm is there?

Comments

Objector 2 alleges that there is no infinite regress, countercharging that being an effect and existing (or being real, *sattva*) are two different things. The concepts have different exclusions (*apoha*). When the sprout is shown to be an effect, we do not have to know that it exists, or is real, in order to know that the seed is its cause. Therefore, no infinite regress gets started. The sprout does not need to be known to be real.

The Nyāya opponent will attempt to answer the countercharge, arguing that an attempt to establish that the pot is known to be a cause does indeed fail to be coherent because of infinite regress.

Text and Translation (p. 71, lines 18–23)

tad asaṅgatam. saty api kāryatvasattvayor vyāvṛttibhede sattāsiddhau kutaḥ kāryatvasiddhiḥ. kāryatvam hy abhūtvābhāvitvam. bhavanam ca sattā. sattā ca saugatānāṃ sāmarthyam eva. tataśca sāmarthyasandehe bhavatīty eva vaktum aśakyam. katham abhūtvābhāvitvaṃ kāryatvaṃ setsyati. apekṣitaparavyāpāratvaṃ kāryatvam ity api nāsato dharmaḥ. sattvaṃ ca sāmarthyam. tac ca sandigdham iti kutaḥ kāryatvasiddhiḥ. tadasiddhau pūrvasya sāmarthyaṃ na sidhyatīti sandigdhāsiddho hetuḥ.

Reply (by objector 1, Bhāsarvajña): That is incoherent. Given that there is indeed difference in the exclusions of "being an effect" and "existence," how (according to you) if existence is not shown is effecthood shown? For, to be an effect is not to be something that does not come to be. And to be is to exist. And existence for you Buddhists is just causal efficiency. And, therefore, if there is doubt about causal efficiency, then it is not possible to say, "It is." How will it be shown that to be an effect is not to be something that does not come to be? To be an effect is to be (the result of) an activity involving another on which it is dependent, while to depend on something is not a property of something non-existent. And existence is causal efficiency (according to you). Given that it is doubtful, how can effecthood be shown? If it is not shown, the efficiency of the earlier is not shown. The prover is therefore unwarranted because it is doubtful.

Comments

The infinite-regress argument is defended against the objection raised. It is true that there is a difference in the exclusions of "existence" and "effecthood"; not everything that is an effect is a real thing. A mirage is not a real thing, but it does seem to be an effect. Nevertheless, on the assumptions connected to Ratnakīrti's argument, there are no non-existent effects; everything that is an effect exists. Here lies the incoherence. That every effect exists follows from the definition of effecthood which requires dependence upon another; a non-existent thing cannot depend on something else. Consequently, given the Buddhist definition of existence as causal efficiency, if there is doubt about the existence of something putatively known as an effect, then it must be shown that it too produces an effect. Infinite regress is unavoidable. There thus remains doubt about whether the pot is causally efficient, and the prover in the inference is thus unwarranted.

Ratnakīrti will show the errors of this reasoning a bit below. Next the opponent puts forth another charge.

Text and Translation (p. 71, lines 24–28)

> *tathā viruddho 'py ayam. tathā hi kṣaṇikatve sati na tāvad ajātasyānanvayaniruddhasya vā kāryārambhakatvaṃ saṃbhavati. na ca niṣpannasya tāvān kṣaṇo 'sti yam upādāya kasmaicit kāryāya vyāpāryeta. ataḥ kṣaṇikapakṣa evārthakriyānupapatter viruddhatā. atha vā vikalpena yad upanīyate tat sarvam avastu. tataś ca vastvātmake kṣaṇikatve sādhye 'vastūpasthāpayann anumānavikalpo viruddhaḥ.*

(Objector 1 continues:) Your prover is also contradictory. For example, on the momentariness premise, originating of an effect is possible, first of all, neither for something unproduced nor for something blocked because of being unconnected (with the effect). And an effect produced cannot have such an (extended) moment in which to operate (and so produce) whatever (new) effect. Therefore, just because of the momentariness thesis, practical production is impossible. This is a contradiction.

Alternatively, what is inferred on the basis of your thesis is that all is unreal (*avastu*, "not a real thing"). And therefore, given that the probandum is momentariness with respect to real things, the inferential option that leads us to cognize an unreal thing is contradictory.

Comments

A prover is contradictory if it occurs only where the probandum is not found. The opponent argues here that only enduring things can have causal efficiency. A momentary thing cannot have causal efficiency before, during, or after production of the effect. Before the effect is produced, the alleged cause cannot have capacity, for the effect is still unproduced. During the production of the effect, the cause is blocked from acting as a producer because, being momentary, it does not exist long enough to be connected to the effect, which does not arise until the next moment. After the effect is produced, the alleged cause cannot have causal efficiency because the effect already exists. The prover in Ratnakīrti's argument is thus contradictory: causal efficiency proves non-momentariness.

The Buddhist might again try to argue that the causal relation is illusory. But if that were so, there would be another contradiction. Ratnakīrti's argument is supposed to prove that everything is momentary, but now it is held that a cause is falsely projected into relation with the effect. The cause is therefore unreal, and this contradicts the initial assumption of the reality of those things that were supposed to be proved momentary.

Text and Translation (p. 71, lines 28–30)

> *yad vā sarvasyaiva hetoḥ kṣaṇikatve sādhye viruddhatvaṃ deśakālāntarānanugame sādhyasādhanabhāvābhavāt. anugame ca nānākālam ekam akṣaṇikaṃ kṣaṇikatvena virudhyata iti.*

(Objector 1 continues:) Or, alternatively, if the prover is everything and the probandum momentariness, there is contradiction in that, given no continuity with another time and place, there can be no correlation between probandum and prover. And if there is continuity, there is something that exists at various times, something that is non-momentary—(a thesis) contradicted by momentariness.

Comments

The opponent charges that the argument is contradictory in other ways. Correlation between prover and probandum is only possible on the basis of repeating properties that occur in various times and places. If everything is momentary, there can be no properties qualifying events at different times and places, and hence there can be no correlations supporting any inference-grounding pervasion. It is contradictory to argue for momentariness on the basis of correlations that cannot exist if things are momentary. On the other hand, if such repeatable entities exist, they would themselves be non-momentary, and this would contradict the intended conclusion of the argument, that all things are momentary.

Text and Translation (p. 72, line 1)

anaikāntiko apy ayam, sattvasthairyayor virodhābhāvād iti.

(Objector 1 continues:) Your prover is also inconclusive, because there is no contradiction between those two (existence and causal efficiency) and things that endure.

Comments

Only a single counterexample is required to show that a prover is inconclusive. The opponent argues that both causal efficiency and existence are inconclusive provers because it is entirely possible that something enduring could exist and be causally efficient.

Text and Translation (p. 72, lines 2–3)

atrocyate. yat tāvad uktaṃ sāmarthyaṃ na pratīyate iti, tat kim sarvathaiva na pratīyate, kṣaṇabhaṅgapakṣe vā.

Ratnakīrti: To this we answer. When you say that the capacity is not cognized (with respect to the example of the pot in our inference), do you mean that it is in no way cognized, or do you mean that it is not cognized only given our view that things are momentary?

Comments

Ratnakīrti now responds to the triple charge that his prover is unwarranted, contradictory, and inconclusive. He begins with the opponent's argument that, because the pot is not known to be causally efficient, the inference from causal efficiency is fallacious in that the prover is unwarranted (see *Text and Translation* p. 71, line 1). Ratnakīrti first asks whether the opponent, our Bhāsarvajña, means that the capacity that is supposed to be cognized as qualifying the pot is entirely beyond knowledge, or whether he means merely that knowledge of capacity is not possible if everything is momentary. Ratnakīrti shall now proceed to show that both options are closed.

Text and Translation (p. 72, lines 4–8)

> *prathamapakṣe sakalakārakajñāpakahetucakrocchedān mukhaspandanamātrasyāpy akaraṇaprasaṅgaḥ. anyathā yenaiva vacanena sāmarthyaṃ nāstīti pratipādyate tasyaiva tatpratipādanasāmarthyam avyāhatam āyātam. tasmāt paramapuruṣārthasamīhayā vastutattvanirūpaṇapravṛttasya śaktisvīkārapūrvikaiva pravṛttiḥ. tadasvīkāre tu na kaścit kvacit pravarteteti nirīhaṃ jagaj jāyeta.*

(Ratnakīrti continues:) Because, on the first option, the wheel of causes (*hetu-cakra*) would be cut off with respect to all knowledge and activity, there would be the bad consequence that there would be no cause even for moving one's mouth. In contrast, the capacity for producing understanding of a statement is arrived at indisputably through whatever statement asserts that there is no capacity. Therefore, the activity of someone who, with eagerness for the highest goal, has set out to determine the truth of things, is invariably preceded by accepting the meaning of words. But if it were not accepted, nobody anywhere could do anything. The world would be without purposeful activity.

Comments

Ratnakīrti considers the first option, that causal capacity, such as is attributed to the pot, is not cognized at all. His refutation is based on pragmatic contradiction. If capacity cannot at all be known, then there would be no reason to expect a causal result from anything, and consequently, no activity in expectation of a certain result. Nor would there be knowledge of anything, which depends in various ways on causal factors. Specifically, there would be no point in asserting anything, including the opponent's own proposition that the pot, the example in Ratnakīrti's inference, fails to have causal capacity. In the very act of denying capacity in general, the objector proves his statement false. The action presupposes both that something has caused the speaker to make the statement and that the statement itself has the capacity to produce understanding in a hearer. Indeed, all purposeful activity has as a prerequisite knowledge of causal capacities, and so denial of cognition of capacity altogether would lead to the obviously mistaken position that there is no purposeful activity.

Text and Translation (p. 72, lines 9–11)

> *atha dvitīyaḥ pakṣaḥ tadāsti tāvat sāmarthyapratītiḥ. sā ca kṣaṇikatve yadi nopapadyate tadā viruddhaṃ vaktum ucitam. asiddham iti tu nyāyabhūṣaṇīyaḥ pāpo vilāpaḥ.*

Objection (by Bhāsarvajña): The second alternative is correct (namely, that causal capacity is impossible only on the assumption that everything is momentary).

Ratnakīrti: First of all, cognition of capacity occurs. And if it is not possible given momentariness, then it would be appropriate to say that our prover is contradictory. However, the objection of the author of the *Nyāyabhūṣaṇa* (Bhāsarvajña) that it is unwarranted is a charge that is practically ridiculous.

Comments

The second option is that capacity is incompatible with the momentariness of things. Ratnakīrti makes clear that he thinks that capacity is known. He agrees that it would be a problem for him if this knowledge were incompatible with momentariness. The prover in his inference would then be contradictory, showing that things are enduring precisely because at least something must endure if we are to cognize the capacity on which the Buddhist argument is based. However, Ratnakīrti intends to give an account of how capacity can be cognized entirely in terms of momentary entities. For this reason, the opponent's complaint can be dismissed, although the story remains to be told.

Text and Translation (p. 72, lines 11–19)

> *na ca saty api kṣaṇikatve sāmarthyapratītivyāghātaḥ. tathā hi kāraṇagrāhijñānopādeyabhūtena kāryagrāhiṇā jñānena tadarpitasaṃskāragarbheṇa asya bhāve asya bhāva ity anvayaniścayo janyate. tathā kāraṇāpekṣayā bhūtalakaivalyagrāhijñānopādeyabhūtena kāryāpekṣayā bhūtalakaivalyagrāhiṇā jñānena tadarpitasaṃskāragarbheṇa asyābhāve asyābhāva iti vyatirekaniścayo janyate. yad āhur guravaḥ –*
>
> > *ekāvasāyasamanantarajātam anyavijñānam anvayavimarśam upādadhāti.*
> >
> > *evaṃ tadekavirahānubhavodbhavānyavyāvṛttidhīḥ prathayati vyatirekabuddhim.*

(Ratnakīrti continues:) And it is not the case that assuming the truth of momentariness there is a contradiction with knowledge of capacity. In particular, a bit of certainty about a positive correlation—namely, that given the presence of the one there is the presence of the other—arises by means of an effect-grasping cognition that has access to the cognition that grasped the cause by being impregnated by a deposited memory disposition (*saṃskāra*) of the cause. Similarly, a bit of certainty about a negative correlation—namely, that given the absence of the one there is the absence of the other—arises by means of an effect-grasping cognition that has access to the cognition that grasped the absence of the cause by being impregnated by a deposited memory disposition of that absence.

So, the "teachers" say: "A second cognition born in immediate correlation with a first opens it to appreciation (*vimarśa*) of a positive correlation. Similarly, thought of the exclusion of one thing arising out of the experience of the absence of another extends it to cognition of negative correlation."

Comments

In order to show that momentariness is compatible with cognition of capacity, Ratnakīrti must give an account of how it is possible that there can be a cognition that grasps both the cause and the effect at the same time. On the assumption that all entities are momentary, it might seem that a current cognition could grasp only a current object. If there are no enduring entities that can serve as a single cognizer of an earlier cause and a later effect, then no story can be told about how causal capacity comes to be known. By the time the effect is cognized, both the cause and the cognition of the cause no longer exist. Thus there would be no access to either one when the effect is cognized.

Ratnakīrti argues that cognition of a causal connection works through the depositing of a trace, or *saṃskāra*, impregnating, so to say, a current cognition with information from the previous cognition. This makes it open to the kind of consideration, or reflection, that is recognized across philosophic schools (Mīmāṃsā, Nyāya, etc.) as crucial for inference. When a person experiences the striking of the match, she forms a memory disposition containing the information present in the experience. If successful striking regularly correlates with experience of fire, cognition of the effect, fire, forces a reflective connection of the two, which is a basis for inference. The *saṃskāra* from the experience of the cause impregnates the current experience of the effect. The information relating to the earlier cognition of the cause is available, not because there is an enduring cognizer, but because the *saṃskāra* faithfully reproduces the information. This allows knowledge of positive correlations. A similar story is told for knowledge of negative correlations.

The "teachers" could be the followers of Prābhākara Mīmāṃsā (Prabhākara himself being referred to across school as "the teacher"). Woo says that he cannot determine who "the teachers" are but presumes they are Buddhist. However, he tells us he has not found the verse in the set of texts he has identified as the most important for Ratnakīrti.[42]

Text and Translation (p. 72, lines 20–23)

> *evaṃ sati gṛhītānusandhāyaka evāyaṃ vikalpaḥ,*
> *upādānopādeyabhūtakramipratyakṣadvayagṛhītānusandhānāt.*
> *yadāhālaṅkāraḥ yadi nāmaikam adhyakṣaṃ na pūrvāparavittimat*
> *adhyakṣadvayasadbhāve prākparāvedanaṃ katham. iti.*

(Ratnakīrti continues:) This being so, we can take the position (make the constuction, *vikalpa*) that there is a grasper of a transtemporal

[42] Woo (1999), p. 181.

connection. Cognition of the transtemporal connection is grasped through two perceptions in a (causal) series where the one (the earlier perception) is accessible to (*upādeya*) that which receives it (*upādāna*) (i.e., the later perception, its effect).

This is the right response to Alaṅkāra's verse: "If there is not a single witness having both the earlier and the later cognitions, how can there be knowledge of both the earlier and later, given the existence (on your view) of two witnesses (one for each cognition)?"

Comments

Ratnakīrti now shows that this method refutes the objection that without an enduring witness knowledge of causal relations is impossible. There is access to the earlier grasping of the cause at the later time of the grasping of the effect. This makes it possible that there be cognition of a transtemporal connection and a cognizer of a transtemporal connection, namely, that cognizer whose cognition of the effect is informed by a *saṃskāra* generated by the earlier cognition of the cause.

We have not been able to determine to whom Ratnakīrti refers with the name "Alaṅkāra," which alternatively may not be a proper name but rather "the aesthete." This could be one of a number of authors who wrote both philosophy and within the tradition of literary aesthetics (*alaṅkāra-śāstra*).

Text and Translation (p. 72, lines 24–29)

> *nāpi dvitīyo 'siddhaprabhedaḥ. sāmarthyaṃ hi sattvam iti saugatānāṃ sthitir eṣā. na caitatprasādhanārtham asmākam idānīm eva prārambhaḥ. kim tu yatra pramāṇapratīte bījādau vastubhūte dharmiṇi pramāṇapratītaṃ sāmarthyaṃ tatra kṣaṇabhaṅgaprasādhanāya. tataś cāṅkurādīnāṃ kāryādarśanād āhatya sāmarthyasandehe 'pi paṭupratyakṣaprasiddham asatparāvṛttaṃ sanmātratvam avāryam eva. anyathāṅkurādau sattāmātrānabhyupagame pratidarśanaṃ lakṣaṇabhedapraṇayanāyogāt. sarvatra sadvyavahārābhāvaprasaṅgāc ca.*

(Ratnakīrti continues:) Our prover also is not unwarranted in a second way. For the Buddhist stance is that capacity is existence. We do not just now begin to say this for our purpose of establishing our view (that all is momentary). Rather, insofar as capacity has been veridically cognized through a knowledge source (*pramāṇa*) with respect to something like a seed that itself has been veridically cognized, it may serve the purpose of proving momentariness.

And, therefore, even in the face of doubt about capacity on the part of a subject who is doubtful about capacity through lack of awareness that there is an effect such as a sprout, it is entirely unavoidable that the thing at least exists. This is well-known by perception of the astute, its non-existence being excluded (perceptually). Otherwise, if you do not admit that the sprout at least exists while you see it, there would be no connection between words and various types (of things such as a cow, a horse, a perception, an inference, and so on), and you would face the bad consequence that in every case there is no connection between conventional speech and what is.

Comments

The opponent charged that Ratnakīrti's argument was unwarranted—specifically, that capacity was not known to qualify the pot—in two different ways. (1) Causal relations are unknowable on the Buddhist view, and (2) the attempt to establish that something has capacity leads to an infinite regress because the effect must also be shown to be capable and so on. Ratnakīrti argues against the second charge here: there is no infinite regress, because once it is known that something exists, we also know that it has capacity, even without seeing its effect. If there is doubt about whether a seed is capable because the sprout is not observed, even if nothing else is known about it, it is at least known to exist. If it is not acknowledged that it exists, then there would be no connection between words and things. One might as well use the word "seed" even when there is no seed; one may use the word "perception" without restrictions. We have other arguments to show that existence is equivalent to capacity. And once you see that, you are ready to see how momentariness follows.

Text and Translation (p. 72, line 29–p. 73, line 2)

> *tasmāc chāstrīyasattvalakṣaṇasandehe 'pi paṭupratyakṣabalāvalambitavastubhāve 'ṅkurādau kāryatvam upalabhyamānaṃ bījādeḥ sāmarthyam upasthāpayatīti nāsiddhidoṣāvakāśaḥ.*

(Ratnakīrti continues:) Therefore, even in the face of dispute about the definition of existence according to (various) *śāstras*, the experience-established fact that things such as a sprout are effects—in their coming to be the things that they are in depending on something else, as is perceived by the astute—shows that things such as the seed have capacity. Thus there is no occasion for the charge that our prover is unwarranted.

Comments

That an existent effect is not self-existent is known by perception. Since this is given, there is no infinite regress. The capacity of the cause explains this dependence, and thus there is no problem establishing it with respect to whatever case is at issue, e.g., our example of a pot. Hence capacity is not unwarranted as a ground for inferring that the pot is momentary.

Text and Translation (p. 73, lines 3–5)

> *nāpi kṣaṇikatve sāmarthyakṣatiḥ, yato viruddhatā syāt. kṣaṇikatvaniyataprāgbhāvitvalakṣaṇakāraṇatvayor virodhābhāvāt kṣaṇamātrasthāyino 'pi sāmarthyasaṃbhavād iti nādimaḥ virodhaḥ.*

(Ratnakīrti continues:) Nor in accepting capacity given momentariness do we incur the harm that thus there would be contradiction: there is no contradiction between momentariness and causality defined as rule-bound (*niyata*) prior existence. Therefore, there is no contradiction of the first kind alleged, because it is possible that even something that remains only for a moment can have capacity.

Comments

The opponent laid out a charge of contradictoriness against Ratnakīrti's inference in two more ways: (1) in order to produce an effect, a cause must endure over time, and (2) an inference requires a universal pervasion involving a connection that extends over time and space. The objection in both cases is that, in order to make the inference for momentariness work, the position of momentariness must be abandoned. Ratnakīrti responds to (1) here, arguing that the cause does not need to endure into the next moment to be connected to the effect. Causality is merely a rule that the effect exists if and only if its cause exists in the preceding moment.

Consequently, a cause does not have to exist at the same time as its effect. There is thus no contradiction between causality and momentariness.

Text and Translation (p. 73, lines 5–7)

> *nāpi dvitīyo virodhaprabhedaḥ. avastuno vastuno vā svākārasya grāhyatve 'pi adhyavaseyavas tv apekṣayaiva sarvatra prāmāṇyapratipādanād vastusvabhāvasyaiva kṣaṇikatvasya siddhir iti kva virodhaḥ.*

(Ratnakīrti continues:) There is also no contradiction of the second kind alleged. Whether an object is real or unreal, its own form (*svākāra*) is grasped nevertheless, i.e., it is something that is determined in thought (*adhyavaseya* and thus fit to feed inference). But then since only through dependence (on such grasping) is there in any instance veridical understanding (understanding based on knowledge sources, *pramāṇa*), where is the contradiction in our proof that connects momentariness just with something's very nature (*svabhāva*)?

Comments

The second kind of contradiction was alleged to result from the truth that a pervasion (all H are S)—which is necessary for inference—would cover cases existing at diverse places and times. Buddhists hold that universals are unreal and that our awareness of universal relationships and use of general terms are constructed through processes by which we see that one particular excludes other particulars. The opponent argued that if the pervasion relationship is grounded in a universal, which is something unreal according to Ratnakīrti then Ratnakīrti's inference cannot give proof with respect to real things. Ratnakīrti responds that it does not matter whether we regard the universal as real or unreal, the inference can function because when a thing is grasped as being of a certain nature, it is conceptualized as having certain universal relations to other particulars. Conceptualization can vary depending on the purposes for which we are grasping the thing. For instance, when we grasp fire, we can conceptualize it as being pervaded by light or by heat depending on whether we are interested in seeing or cooking. Although the pervasion is not based upon an enduring universal present in all instances, each individual fire is nonetheless accompanied by individual occurrences of light and heat. We do not need to grasp a real universal in order to make the inference. We merely need to have a certain conceptualization of the individual thing according to some constructed concept (like fire). Along with that comes a conception of pervasion, given that correlations are observed with respect to other things conceptualized by a similar process. There is thus no contradiction because we can account for the grasping of a pervasion entirely on the basis of momentary entities.

Text and Translation (p. 73, lines 8–17)

> *yac ca gṛhyate yac cādhyavasīyate te dve 'py anyanivṛttī na vastunī, svalakṣaṇāvagāhitve 'bhilāpasaṃsargānupapatter iti cet. na. adhyavasāyasvarūpāparijñānāt. agṛhīte 'pi vastuni mānasyādipravṛttikārakatvaṃ vikalpasyādhyavasāyitvam. apratibhāse 'pi pravṛttiviṣayīkṛtatvam adhyavaseyatvam. etaccādhyavaseyatvaṃ svalakṣaṇasyaiva yujyate, nānyasya. arthakriyārthitvād arthipravṛtteḥ. evaṃ cādhyavasāye svalakṣaṇasyāsphuranam eva. na ca tasyāsphurane 'pi sarvatrāviśeṣeṇa pravṛttyākṣepaprasaṅgaḥ, pratiniyatasāmagrīprasūtāt, pratiniyatasvākārāt, pratiniyataśaktiyogāt, pratiniyata evātadrūpaparāvṛtte 'pratīte 'pi pravṛttisāmarthyadarśanāt, yathā sarvasyāsattve 'pi bījād aṅkurasyaivotpattiḥ, dṛṣṭasya niyatahetuphalabhāvasya pratikṣeptum aśakyatvāt. paraṃ bāhyenārthena sati pratibandhe prāmāṇyam. anyathā tv aprāmāṇyam iti viśeṣaḥ.*

Objection: Although these two, "what is grasped" and "what is conceptualized," have different exclusions, they are not two (distinct) things, because (according to you) it is not possible to have a relation between speech and a fathoming of the self-characterized particular (*svalakṣaṇa*).

Ratnakīrti: Wrong. For the particulars' own nature (*svarūpa*) need not be cognized when there is conceptualization. The mind can make an initial effort towards something even when it has not been grasped: this is what it is to be determined in thought. Even when something has not appeared, it can be something determined in thought, i.e., conceptualized, in being made the object of effort to speak or act (*pravṛtti*). And this being conceptualized is appropriately used indeed with respect to the self-characterized particular, not of another. For effort to speak or act on the part of anyone who wants something is due to the ability of that something to fulfill a purpose (*artha-kriyā*).

And so in this way, given its conceptualization, the self-characterized particular does not show itself completely. Moreover, though it does not thus show itself, there is not the bad consequence that effort is expended indiscriminately in all cases. For the rule-bound (*pratiniyata*) total collection of causes produces the effect, because its own nature is rule-bound in that the appropriateness of capacity is rule-bound. It is indeed rule-bound, even though there be no awareness of the exclusion of what it is not, since efficacy of effort is seen. So even though something is non-existent, there is production just of a sprout from a seed, since it is impossible to deny the observed fact that an effect follows rule-bound from its cause. The superior view, given the blocking of your objection by the external object, is established by *pramāṇa*. Otherwise, there would no establishment through a "knowledge source" (i.e., through inference). This is the difference.

Comments

The opponent tries to cast doubt upon Ratnakīrti's distinction between grasping (*gṛhyate*) a thing and conceptualizing (*adhyavasīyate*) it. Ratnakīrti answers that they are two different things because we can conceptualize something without grasping it. Indeed, an act of making effort toward something unperceived is guided by our desires and purposes. For instance, if a person wants a mango when he is hungry, he must conceptualize the mango as food before checking the fruitbasket. Such conceptualization trails presumptions of many pervasions along with it, such as that between food and hunger satisfaction. A mango to be eaten is absolutely particular and unlike any other, but for the purpose of satisfying hunger a person is interested only in conceptualizing it as food. Whenever anything is grasped, it is conceptualized in some way or another. We never grasp the full particularity of anything. Rather, we project upon it concepts that connect up with other concepts. In this way, despite the fact that the groupings are merely constructions based upon our purposes, we can proceed with inferences based upon these groupings.

The invariable rule with respect to something it is appropriate to call *capable by its own nature* is that when something completely capable exists, its effect comes about. Ratnakīrti has argued that all capable things are momentary. There is no contradiction in that argument because the pervasion it depends on is grounded in momentary entities so conceived without recourse to enduring universals. So it does not matter that universals do not really exist. The causal relation between sprout and seed must be accepted, because we observe production of sprout from seed. If this is denied, then there can be no inference. The *pramāṇa* breaks down.

Text and Translation (p. 73, lines 18–24)

> *tathā tṛtīyo 'pi pakṣaḥ prayāsaphalaḥ. nānākālasyaikasya vastuno vastuto 'saṃbhave 'pi sarvadeśakālavartinor atadrūpaparāvṛttayor eva sādhyasādhanayoḥ pratyakṣeṇa vyāptigrahaṇāt. dvividho hi pratyakṣasya viṣayaḥ grāhyo 'dhyavaseyaś ca. sakalātadrūpaparāvṛttaṃ vastumātraṃ sāksād asphuraṇāt pratyakṣasya grāhyo viṣayo mā bhūt, tadekadeśagrahaṇe tu tanmātrayor vyāptiniścāyakavikalpajananād adhyavaseyo viṣayo bhavaty eva. kṣaṇagrahaṇe santānaniścayavat. rūpamātragrahaṇe rūparasagandhasparśātmakaghaṭaniścayavac ca. anyathā sarvānumānocchedaprasaṅgāt.*

(Ratnakīrti continues:) Similarly, through exertion (of thought), the third objection also leads to the (same) result (namely, that there is no contradiction). For, pervasion of a prover by a probandum is grasped by perception so long as the *exclusion* of each from what it is not extends to all times and places—granted that it is impossible for a single thing really to exist at various times. For the object of perception is of two kinds: (1) what is to be (immediately) grasped (*grāhya*) and (2) what is to be conceptualized (*adhyavaseya*). As a mere thing, an object excludes everything that it is not, because it is grasped immediately in that it does not show itself (as conceptualized). Do not think that the conceptualized object of perception is to be grasped immediately. But given a grasping of it at a single place, the object is conceptualized from the generating of well-grounded conceptions of pervasion between two that are merely such (as we have explained, namely, exclusions). It is like certainty about a series (*santāna*), though grasping is momentary. It is like the certainty that the pot has color, taste, texture, and smell, though only color is grasped. Otherwise, there is the bad consequence of the cutting off of all inference.

Comments

The opponent also argued that Ratnakīrti falls into yet another kind of contradiction when he assumes that there are pervasions capable of grounding inference. Since pervasions are between properties occurring at different places and times, those properties must be able to exist at various times and places. This demand contradicts the intended conclusion of Ratnakīrti's argument, namely, that everything is momentary. In response, Ratnakīrti elaborates his previous argument that there is no contradiction between pervasion and momentariness. Now he explicitly spells out how the pervasion relationship can be epistemically grounded entirely on the basis of momentary entities.

The momentary entity is to be understood in two ways: it is grasped immediately as an absolute particular (a mere thing) without any classification. Such an absolute particular (*svalakṣaṇa*) excludes everything else, because it is absolutely unique. It is also the object of a conceptualization where it is grouped with other things according to our purposes and our system of classification. This conceptualized object is not the object of immediate perception (*nirvikalpaka*); it is the object of determinate perception (*savikalpaka*). As conceptualized, it does not exclude everything else, but only those things that do not have the feature in which we are interested. In this way, it is grouped with other things whose exclusions are the same with respect to the relevant property.

A particular bit of smoke is grouped with other non-smoke-excluding things, and all of these are also non-fire-excluding things. The pervasion is based entirely on particulars conceptualized as qualified by universal properties that are themselves merely constructs based upon common exclusions among particulars. In a similar way, we can construct the idea of a series of momentary particulars, even though our grasping and what we grasp occur only in the present. Only one pot-moment is grasped at a time, but each one is conceptualized under the concept "pot." This implies that it has certain relations to other particular pot-moments, such that they form a common series.

In much the same way, we construct the idea of the pot as having both texture and color, even though only its color is experienced. When we perceive the color of the pot from a distance, we conceptualize it as the color of a pot. It is part of our concept of pots—built up from many previous experiences of particular pots—that they have texture. Consequently, when we grasp a bit of color and conceptualize it is as the color of a pot, we cannot help but also form a bit of certainty that texture is also present, and this leads to the idea of the pot as a single thing having both color and texture. The series, the common-property bearer, and the universal thus all have the same status as constructions, "convenient fictions," based on our experience of momentary particulars.

Text and Translation (p. 73, lines 25–26)

> *tathā hi vyāptigrahaḥ sāmānyayoḥ, viśeṣayoḥ, sāmānyaviśiṣṭasvalakṣaṇayoḥ svalakṣaṇaviśiṣṭasāmānyayor veti vikalpāḥ.*

(Ratnakīrti continues:) Furthermore, grasping can be of a pervasion as holding (1) between two universals (*sāmānya*), (2) between two particulars (*viśeṣa*), (3) between two self-characterized particulars (*svalakṣaṇa*) qualified by universals, or (4) between two universals qualified by self-characterized particulars. These are the options.

Comments

Ratnakīrti considers four different ways of understanding pervasion. The first is the Nyāya view that pervasion is between two universals, such as smokehood and firehood. The second is the impossible view attributed to the Buddhists by their opponents, that two particulars pervade one another even though each is restricted to its own place and time. The third and fourth views are hybrid views. On the third, particulars pervade one another as qualified by universals. On the fourth, pervasion is between universals, but the universals are qualified by particulars. Ratnakīrti's view is a version of this fourth alternative. He now proceeds to reject each of the others.

Text and Translation (p. 73, line 27–p. 74 line 1)

> *nādyo vikalpaḥ, sāmānyasya bādhyatvāt. abādhyatve 'py adṛśyatvāt. dṛśyatve 'pi puruṣārthānupayogitayā tasyānumeyatvāyogāt. nāpy anumitāt sāmānyād viśeṣānumānam. sāmānyasarvasvalakṣaṇayor vakṣyamānanyāyena pratibandhapratipatter ayogāt. nāpi dvitīyaḥ, viśeṣasyānanugāmitvāt.*

(Ratnakīrti continues:) It is not the first option (1), because the universal is defeated (and ruled out). Even if not defeated, then (the first option is wrong) because no universal is fit to be seen. Even if it were fit to be seen, since it is not suitable for the fulfillment of human purposes, it would not be suitable to be the object of someone's inference. Also, it is not the case that from an inferred universal there could be inference to a particular. (The first option is also wrong) because understanding of an opposition between a universal and all particulars is impossible, by an argument to be stated.

It is also not the second option (2), because a particular does not recur.

Comments

Ratnakīrti rejects the first two alternatives. He rejects the first option because universals do not exist. He gives several reasons for this. He argues first of all that universals are not perceived. They are also, he continues, incapable of fulfilling human purposes. Water can quench thirst, but waterhood cannot. Consequently, a universal cannot be inferred, because we only carry out inferences with respect to things that fulfill a purpose. If a universal could be inferred, the process would be useless as a way of inferring something about a particular. For instance, when I infer fire on the mountain, I am not interested in firehood, but in the particular fire that is on the mountain. The pervasion ultimately must be grounded in particulars and not universals or else inferences could not be sources of knowledge to guide action for intended results.

Ratnakīrti admits that the second option is untenable, as the opponent has charged, because the particular's existence is restricted to a single time and place. This rejection of the naive portrayal of the Buddhist position opens the door to the correct view, which has to be phrased more carefully.

Text and Translation (p. 74, lines 2–5)

antime tu vikalpadvaye sāmānyādhāratayā dṛṣṭa eva viśeṣaḥ sāmānyasya viśeṣyo viśeṣanaṃ vā karttavyaḥ. adṛṣṭa eva vā deśakālāntaravartī. yad vā dṛṣṭādṛṣṭātmako deśakālāntarvarttyatadrūpaparāvṛttaḥ sarvo viśeṣaḥ. na prathamaḥ pakṣo 'nanugāmitvāt. nāpi dvitīyaḥ, adṛṣṭatvāt.

(Ratnakīrti continues:) But with respect to the last option (4), there are two (further) choices (to begin with). (4a) The particular is seen indeed to support the universal; it belongs to the universal itself either as (4a1) qualificandum or (4a2) qualifier. (4b) The particular is not seen indeed (to support the universal), being situated (in its full particularity) at another time and place. Or (4c, a third choice), every particular has the character of both being seen (to support the universal) and not being seen as occurring in a particular time and place, excluding what it is not (namely, everything but itself).

It is not the first case (4a), because it (the particular) does not recur. It is also not the second (4b), (just) because it is not seen.

Comments

There are several ways of interpreting the fourth alternative, two of which here are refuted. On the fourth option, pervasion is said to hold between two universals, universals that are qualified by particulars. The qualification relation could have either the particular or the universal as what is qualified and the other as the qualifier. Suboption (4a2) is unusual: the directionality of the qualification relation is a reversal of the usual way philosophers speak (e.g., from Nyāya and Mīmāṃsā), namely, that particulars are qualified by universals, not universals by particulars. Suboption (4a1) is the standard view except that, in addition to the "support" the particular is said to provide, our text reads that the particular "belongs to" the universal. Usually "belonging to" also reverses the terms. In any case, universals stand in pervasion relations while being bound up with particulars. The problem with this view is, Ratnakīrti says flatly with no elaboration, that particulars do not recur. The idea seems to be that there would be a relational mismatch: only something that recurs could relate to a universal in the required way since universals extend to multiple spaces and times.

On the second formulation (4b), universals stand in pervasion relationships without being related to particulars. Particulars do not support univerals since particulars are unique. This view is a non-starter just because knowledge is about particulars and pervasion fails to render the connection needed in order learn about some bit, e.g., of actual fire (*That* fire on *this* mountain, since smokehood is pervaded by firehood and we see some smoke over there).

Ratnakīrti appears to prefer another subformulation (4c) as the proper way to understand the fourth alternative. Universals are qualified by particulars in the sense that they are constructed out of particulars in a process of conceptualization shaped by our desires and purposes, what we need to see things as. Particulars are grouped together according to their relevant exclusions of other particulars, those, namely, that do not fall under some conventional concept tied to our practical purposes. It is these constructed universals that stand in the pervasion relationship. Particulars are conceptualized as falling under such universals, and so pervasion is understood in a way that information about particulars can be conveyed. For instance, S knows that this bit of smoke excludes all non-fiery things because of the way S conceptualizes the thing as smoky. S, along with others in the community, constructs an idea of the universal smokiness out of experience of some of the many particulars that fall under it. This universal, as qualified by the particular bits of smoke, is pervaded by fieriness as qualified by all the particular bits of fire. Hence S knows that this bit of smoke also excludes all particular non-fiery things. There is thus some particular fire that goes along with this particular bit of smoke.

Ratnakīrti has skipped the third option to talk about the fourth which is complex. Now he returns to rule out option (3).

Text and Translation (p. 74, lines 5–6)

> *na ca tṛtīyaḥ, prastutaikaviśeṣadarśane 'pi deśakālāntaravartināṃ viśeṣāṇāṃ adarśanāt.*

(Ratnakīrti continues:) It is not the third option (3), because given that experience is just of one particular in focus, there is no experience of particulars existing at other times and places.

Comments

Ratnakīrti rejects the third option, that it is particulars qualified by universals that stand in the pervasion relation. This view is ruled out because the particular cannot be qualified by a real universal. Nor can a particular be qualified by other particulars with which it is grouped, because these, existing at other times and places, are not experienced. Experience presents particulars but not their classifications.

Text and Translation (p. 74, lines 7–15)

> *atha teṣāṃ sarveṣām eva viśeṣāṇāṃ sadṛśatvāt, sadṛśasāmagrīprasūtatvāt, sadṛśakāryakāritvād iti. pratyāsattyā ekaviśeṣagrāhakaṃ pratyakṣam atadrūpaparāvṛttamātre niścayaṃ janayad atadrūpaparāvṛttaviśeṣamātrasya vyavasthāpakam. yathaikasāmagrīpratibaddharūpamātragrāhakaṃ pratyakṣaṃ*

ghaṭe niścayaṃ janayad ghaṭagrāhakaṃ vyavasthāpyate. anyathā ghaṭo 'pi ghaṭasantāno 'pi pratyakṣato na sidhyet, sarvātmanā grahaṇābhāvāt. tadekadeśagrahaṇaṃ tv atadrūpaparāvṛtte 'py aviśiṣṭam. yady evam anenaiva krameṇa sarvasya viśeṣasya viśeṣaṇaviśeṣyabhāvavad vyāptipratipattir apy astu. tat kim arthaṃ nānākālam ekam akṣaṇikam abhyupagantavyaṃ yena kṣaṇikatvasādhanasya viruddhatvaṃ syād iti na kaścid virodhaprabhedaprasaṅgaḥ.

(Ratnakīrti continues:) In sum, because similarity holds between each and every particular, because production occurs from total collections of causes which are similar, (and) because similar effects are produced, a perception grasping through a sensory connection a single particular produces a bit of certainty specifically about the exclusion of what the thing is not. This establishes that just that particular excludes what it is not. For example, a perception that grasps color specifically, color that is connected to a total collection of causes, produces certainty with respect to a pot. The certainty is established as grasping the pot. Otherwise, even though the thing is a pot, (or, as we would say) a pot-series (*ghaṭa-santāna*), that it is so would not be proved by perception, because it would not be grasped as anything.

However, the grasping of something in a single place is not (a cognition of it as) qualified (by what the thing excludes) even though it does exclude what it is not. If this is so, then it should be accepted that through the sequence (of perception of a particular coming to include exclusions) there is cognition of pervasion of every (similar) particular—at least no less than it should be accepted that there is a relation between qualifier and qualificandum.

Therefore, what is the point of insisting that some single non-momentary thing existing at various times (and places) is to be accepted whereby there would be contradiction of our prover with momentariness? Thus no bad consequence (for our position) is due to any kind of contradiction.

Comments

Ratnakīrti summarizes his refutation of the charge that his inference is contradictory. It is possible to construct the idea of pervasion out of groups of particulars, which, being conceptualized in a certain way, exclude the same things. Such similarity is grounded in causal relations; similar causes produce similar effects. Thus it is possible to say of every particular in a certain group (e.g., bits of smoke) that it has a cause which, through its exclusions, can be grouped with other causes of similar effects (e.g., particular fires). Extrapolation renders cognition of pervasion (e.g., every particular bit of smoke is caused by some particular bit of fire). There does not need to be any smokehood or firehood as single entities occurring at various times. There is thus no need to posit enduring entities to ground inference, and there is consequently no contradiction between momentariness and the possibility of inference.

Text and Translation (p. 74, lines 16–17)

> *na cāyam anaikāntiko 'pi hetuḥ, pūrvoktakrameṇa*
> *sādharmyadṛṣṭānte prasaṅgaviparyayahetubhyām*
> *anvayarūpavyāpteḥ prasādhanāt.*

(Ratnakīrti continues:) Furthermore, our prover is not inconclusive, because, by the sequence stated earlier, the pervasion is made known in the form of a positive correlation: the positive example is obtained by two provers, a *prasaṅga* and its transformation.

Comments

Ratnakīrti addresses the charge that the inference is "inconclusive" in the technical sense that there are known counterexamples insofar as the prover is known to occur both where the probandum is and where it is not. Ratnakīrti appears to admit that there is no undisputed example of a momentary thing. The pot mentioned in the main inference is not obviously something that does not endure. However, Ratnakīrti reminds us that he has given an independent argument that establishes the pot as momentary and thus establishes an instance of positive correlation between existence and momentariness. Unless the opponent can find an undisputed counterexample or can refute the supporting argument referred to here, there is no reason why our prover, existence, should be considered inconclusive. The supporting argument consisted of inferences comprising a *prasaṅga* and its transformation. (See above: *Text and Translation* p. 67, line 23 through p. 68, line 24.)

Text and Translation (p. 74, lines 17–20)

> *nanu yadi prasaṅgaviparyayahetudvayabalato ghaṭe dṛṣṭānte kṣaṇabhaṅgaḥ sidhyet tadā sattvasya niyamena kṣaṇikatvena vyāptisiddher anaikāntikatvaṃ na syād iti yuktam. kevalam idam evāsambhavi. tathā hi śakto 'pi ghaṭaḥ kramikasahakāryapekṣayā kramikāryaṃ kariṣyati.*

Objection: If destruction in a moment were established with respect to the example of the pot by force of two provers, a *prasaṅga* and its transformation, then it would be correct that the proof of pervasion of existence by momentariness according to a rule would not be inconclusive. However, what is impossible is precisely this. In other words, even though the pot is capable, it will produce an effect in a sequence through its dependence on a sequence of auxiliary causes (*kramika-saha-kārin*).

Comments

The opponent admits that if Ratnakīrti's pair of supporting arguments were sound, the momentariness of the pot would be proved, the pervasion would be established, and the prover would not be inconclusive. However, he says here, the supporting arguments are not sound. Something can have the capacity to produce something else without actually producing the thing. Ratnakīrti argued above that if something can be appropriately spoken of as producing, then it must produce right then and there. Thus an enduring thing with a variety of capacities would have to produce all its effects at once and at every moment of its existence—contrary to both observation and reason. The opponent now rejoins that a thing can produce its effects sequentially: the production of each effect depends upon auxiliary causes that arrive in sequence. The stock example is a seed that requires the auxiliaries of soil and water, etc., to sprout. So something can have multiple capacities, dispositional properties or relations that are triggered by other factors in a total collection of causes, such that, for example, different people can all have experience of the same thing (the thing being a causal factor in many different causal chains). Though something has all of its capacities constantly, it produces its effects sequentially, as the auxiliary causes arrive on the scene.

Text and Translation (p. 74, lines 21–22)

> *na caitad vaktavyam. samartho 'rthaḥ svarūpeṇa karoti. svarūpaṃ ca sarvadāstīty anupakāriṇī sahakāriṇy apekṣā na yujyata iti.*

Ratnakīrti: That should not be said. The capable object produces by its own nature (by its "own form," *svarūpa*). Its own nature is always what it is without assistance. It is not appropriately said to depend on auxiliary causes.

Comments

Ratnakīrti repeats his earlier reason for rejecting auxiliary causes. If something is capable of producing by its own nature (*svarūpa*), then in that it needs no assistance to have its own nature it should not require outside help to produce.

Text and Translation (p. 74, lines 22–26)

> *saty api svarūpeṇa kārakatve sāmarthyābhāvāt kathaṃ karotu. sahakārisākalyaṃ hi sāmarthyam. tadvaikalyaṃ cāsāmarthyam. na ca tayor āvirbhāvatirobhāvābhyāṃ tadvataḥ kācit kṣatiḥ, tasya tābhyām anyatvāt. tasmād arthaḥ samartho 'pi syāt, na ca karotīti sandigdhavyatirekaḥ prasaṅgahetuḥ.*

Objection: Even though something is a cause by its own nature, how could it produce without capacity? For capacity is the entire collection of auxiliary factors; what is deficient is incapable. Something having that (i.e., causal productivity) does not lose it through the appearance and disappearance of the two (capacity and incapacity), because it (causal productivity) is other than those two (capacity and incapacity). Therefore, a capable object too could be something that does not produce. Thus there is doubt about the negative correlation supporting your prover derived from the (alleged) *prasaṅga*.

Comments

The opponent tries to draw a distinction between causality (*kārakatva*) and capacity (*sāmarthya*). If something has causality by its own nature, it does not necessarily produce immediately. Rather, it produces only in the presence of auxiliary causes. Capacity, however, is equivalent to an entire collection of auxiliary causes (*saha-kāri-sākalya*) being present.

The collection is sufficient for the effect. Consequently, a thing can be a cause by its own nature without producing, due to the absence of one or another auxiliary cause. Therefore, something that is capable (*samartha*) in the broadest sense of being a cause (*karakatva*) might not produce its effect immediately. There is thus a counterexample to the negative correlation, "Whatever does not produce is not capable," namely, something that is a cause by its very nature but that does not produce immediately because of the absence of some auxiliary cause.

Text and Translation (p. 74, line 27–p. 75, line 4)

> *atrocyate. bhavatu tāvat sahakārisākalyam eva sāmarthyam. tathāpi so 'pi tāvad bhāvaḥ svarūpeṇa kārakaḥ. tasya ca yādṛśaś caramakṣaṇe 'kṣepakriyādharmo*[43] *svabhāvas tādṛśa eva cet prathamakṣaṇe tadā tadāpi prasahya kurvāṇo brahmaṇāpy anivāryaḥ. na ca so 'py akṣepakriyādharmo*[44] *svabhāvaḥ sākalye sati jāto bhāvād bhinna evābhidhātuṃ śakyaḥ, bhāvasyākartṛtvaprasaṅgāt. evaṃ yāvad yāvad dharmāntaraparikalpas tāvat tāvad udāsīno bhāvaḥ. tasmād yadrūpam ādāya svarūpeṇāpi janayatīty ucyate tasya prāg api bhāve katham ajaniḥ kadācit. akṣepakriyāpratyanīkasvabhāvasya vā prācyasya paścād anuvṛttau kathaṃ kadācid api kāryasaṃbhavaḥ.*

Ratnakīrti: To this we answer. First of all, let capacity be understood to be nothing other than the entire collection of auxiliary factors. Nevertheless, whatever is existent (including such a collection) is a cause by its own nature. If belonging to such a thing—whose property is to produce without delay at the last moment—there be a self-nature of just that sort (i.e., to produce), then, being capable from the first moment (that it is capable), it produces at that time; such is not preventable even by the Absolute Brahman.

Moreover, it cannot be held that a self-nature (*svabhāva*) whose property it is to produce without delay when there is a complete collection of causes would itself arise as a thing distinct from its existence

---

[43] Reading *dharmo* instead of *dharmā*.

[44] Reading *dharmo* instead of *dharmā*.

(*bhāva*) which would be produced given the whole collection: the unfortunate consequence would be that an existing thing does not act.

In this way, whatever thought you may have of another property, you could think of its existence only as inactive (*udāsīna*, and thus as non-existent). Therefore, it is to be accepted that whatever form is in focus (as producing, such as a seed) produces by its own nature. How could it be existent while non-producing at any time before that? In other words, how could something with a self-nature opposed to immediate action come to have an effect afterwards, after being the former thing (that did not have the effect) such that it would be continuously the same thing?

Comments

Ratnakīrti argues that the attempt to draw a distinction between causality and capacity does not affect his argument. Even if we accept that something only has capacity when the total collection of causal factors is present, that very collection must still be a cause by its own nature. Something that is a cause by its own nature must produce without delay. If the thing is rightly conceived as having that nature before the arrival of its last ingredient, so to say, nothing could prevent it from producing at the earlier time. The fact that something imagined does not produce earlier shows simply that it is non-existent. That is not the thing that exists when the final factor arrives. To expunge the metaphor and use the more precise language of moments and series: only the last member of a series that exists, itself fed by a complexity of causal auxiliaries, is actually the cause of any effect in focus.

Ratnakīrti sees his opponent as trying to conceive of a self-nature of thing (*svabhāva*) as distinct from its existence (*bhāva*), but that is impossible. Nothing can exist without producing something else. It must have whatever nature it has whenever it exists. If that is to be the cause of a certain effect, it must produce the effect. One and the same entity cannot have the self-nature of producing the effect and not producing it. If an enduring entity ever had the nature of not producing the effect, it could not acquire that nature without ceasing to be the former thing.

Text and Translation (p. 75, lines 5–9)

> *nanu yadi sa evaikaḥ kartā syād yuktam etad. kiṃ tu sāmagrī janikā. tataḥ sahakāryantaravirahavelāyāṃ balīyaso 'pi na*

kāryaprasava iti kim atra viruddham. na hi bhāvaḥ svarūpeṇa karotīti svarūpeṇaiva karoti, sahakārisahitād eva tataḥ kāryotpattidarśanāt. tasmād vyāptivat kāryakāraṇabhāvo 'py ekatrānyayogavyavacchedenānyatrāyogavyacchedenāvabod-dhavyaḥ, tathaiva laukikaparīkṣakāṇāṃ saṃpratipatter iti.

Objection: If the producer were just a single thing, this would be correct. But the producer is the total collection of causes (*sāmagrī*, the collection that is "sufficient" for the effect). Therefore, on the occasion of a lack of one or another auxiliary cause (in the bundle that makes up the *sāmagrī*), even the very powerful does not produce the effect. So what in this is contradictory? For when we say "An entity produces by its own nature," it is not that it produces by that nature alone, because it is seen that production of the effect comes from it only when it is connected with auxiliary causes. Therefore, like pervasion, a causal relation too is to be determined through specification of the connection of one thing to another and its non-connection to others. In just this way, both average people and specialists have a common understanding.

Comments

The opponent admits that Ratnakīrti's reasoning would be correct if the producer were just one single thing which would either have the capacity or not at any given moment. However, the Buddhist has articulated the concept of the total collection of causal factors, *sāmagrī*, which is the actual producer. If a single causal factor is lacking, there may be something that is almost powerful enough to produce the effect on its own and yet the effect is not produced. For instance, when a seed is in the ground with warmth and all the auxiliary factors present except water, no sprout is produced. The seed, earth, air, sunlight combination is insufficient. A seed produces a sprout by its own nature, but it does not produce it without help. Thus its having the nature of being a cause of a sprout is determined by the fact that it produces a sprout when joined with certain things and not when joined with others. Causality is not immediate production, but production under certain conditions. This is the way causes are talked about, both in everyday speech and when we are engaged in metaphysical argument.

Text and Translation (p. 75, lines 10–14)

> *atrocyate. yadā militāḥ santaḥ kāryaṃ kurvate tadaikārthakaraṇalakṣaṇaṃ sahakāritvam eṣām astu, ko niṣeddhā. militair eva tu tat kāryaṃ karttavyam iti kuto labhyate. pūrvāparayor ekasvabhāvatvād bhāvasya sarvadā jananājananayor anyataraniyamaprasaṅgasya durvāratvāt. tasmāt sāmagrī janikā, naikaṃ janakam iti sthiravādināṃ manorathasyāpy aviṣayaḥ.*

Ratnakīrti: To this we answer. If it is as united (*milita*) that they produce the effect, then let it be granted that they have auxiliary-cause status, which is to be defined with respect to the producing of a single thing—who would deny this? But why is it that the effect is produced only by them united? (A single cause, a unique and total union of auxiliaries, is to be identified as producing the effect.) You cannot avoid the bad consequence of the rule that an entity at all times either produces or does not produce, since the earlier and the later each have a single nature (differing in virtue of their differing capacities). Therefore the total collection of causal factors (*sāmagrī*) is the producer (and it is a single thing); the view that there is not a single producer is impossible however much it is desired by advocates of endurance.

Comments

Ratnakīrti rushes to affirm that things brought together into a causal collection sufficient for an effect may be granted the status of causal auxiliary. The opponent's mistake does not lie here. It depends instead on the premise that the plurality of factors is the producer of the effect while remaining a plurality. The truth is that a plurality of factors have to come together (*milita*), i.e., have to unite, in order to produce. The total collection of factors as a single thing produces the effect as a single thing. Something that produces at any given time is different from something that does not. Since it is only when the causal factors are united that the effect is produced, we should speak of that union, which is a single thing, as the producer. A single effect is not most immediately produced by a plurality of producers—that view misses the crucial point of the necessity of their coming together—but by something itself single.

Text and Translation (p. 75, lines 15–19)

> *dṛśyate tāvad idam iti cet dṛśyatām. kiṃ tu pūrvasthitād eva sāmagrīmadhyapraviṣṭād bhāvāt kāryotpattir anyasmād eva vā viśiṣṭād bhāvād utpannād iti vivādapadam. tatra prāg api saṃbhave sarvadaiva kāryotpattir na vā kadācid apīti virodham asamādhāya cakṣuṣī nimīlya tata eva kāryotpattidarśanād iti sādhyānuvādamātrapravṛttaḥ kṛpām arhatīti.*

Objection: What you say is found (but that is our view).

Ratnakīrti: (Yes) it should be found. However, the item in dispute is whether the production of the effect is (1) from a thing existing previously that has entered into the middle of a collection of factors or (2) only from a second thing, something distinct (from that collection as a plurality, namely, a unity) that is (itself) produced. Concerning this question, if something can produce at the prior time, then it should produce the effect all the time or never (otherwise it would not be one and the same thing). You who do not appreciate this contradiction have to shut your eyes to it; only then can you see the production of the effect. Have pity on a person who merely continues to repeat what needs to be proved!

Comments

Ratnakīrti clarifies the issue by identifying the crucial question as how to interpret the causal process. The opponent has admitted that it is a union of factors that is the producer. Now imagine that all the factors for production of some effect are present excepting some final factor or "trigger." The final causal factor arrives and the effect is produced. There are two theories about how to view the triggering: (1) the endurance theory, which holds that the adding of the trigger to the bundle allows an enduring cause to exercise its capacity; and (2) the momentariness theory, which holds that the final factor arises as capable because it arises as joined with the others. The problem with the endurance theory is that the main cause—e.g., the seed—does not have causal capacity until the trigger arrives. If such a thing would have its essential property of producing the effect even before it is joined with the others, it should produce at the earlier time. If it does not produce then, then it can never produce even when joined with the others at the risk of losing its nature, its identity. Only if we ignore this argument does it make sense to hold the endurance theory. The heart of the Ratnakīrti's position is this argument about identity and change, as will become progressively clear.

Text and Translation (p. 75, lines 20–22)

> *na ca pratyabhijñādibalād ekatvasiddhiḥ. tatpaurūṣasya lūnapunarjātakeśanakhādāv apy upalambhato nirdalanāt. lakṣaṇabhedasya ca darśayitum aśakyatvāt. sthirasiddhidūṣaṇe*[45] *cāsmābhiḥ prapañcato nirastatvāt.*

(Ratnakīrti continues:) And it is not the case that unity (over time) is established through the force of recognition (*pratyabhijña*, "This is that Devadatta whom I saw previously") and the like. This holds because: (1) personal experience can be unbroken even when (change of characteristics creates new identities, i.e., when) hair, nails, etc., are cut off and regrow; (2) (in so-called recognition) distinctive characteristics (of the later thing) are not experienced; and (3) the view has been rejected by us as elaborated in detail in the *Sthirasiddhidūṣaṇa*.

Comments

Ratnakīrti rebuts again the objection that recognition proves the existence of an enduring thing. When a person sees Devadatta for a second time, she experiences no distinction between the two because she fails to see any differentiating characteristics. However, Devadatta will doubtless have changed. His hair, for instance, may have been cut and regrown. Such considerations show that the experience of recognition can occur even where the perceived object ("This Devadatta") and the object remembered ("that Devadatta whom I saw previously") are different. There is consequently no pervasion between recognition and the identity of that "recognized." Ratnakīrti directs us to his *Sthirasiddhidūṣaṇa* for a more elaborate discussion of the reasoning.

Text and Translation (p. 75, lines 22–26)

> *tasmāt sākṣāt kāryakāraṇabhāvāpekṣayobhayatrāpy anyayogavyavacchedaḥ. vyāptau tu sākṣāt paramparayā kāraṇamātrāpekṣayā kāraṇe vyāpake 'yogavyavacchedaḥ. kārye*

[45] Reading *sthirasiddhidūṣaṇe* instead of *sthirasiddhadūṣaṇe*.

vyāpye 'nyayogavyavacchedaḥ. tathā tadatadsvabhāve vyāpake 'yogavyavacchedaḥ. tatsvabhāve ca vyāpye 'nyayogavyavacchedaḥ. vikalpārūḍharūpāpekṣayā vyāptau dvividham avadhāraṇam.

(Ratnakīrti continues:) Therefore, it is clear that with respect to the cause and effect relationship, irrespective of the direction of the relationship, the relationship is to be specified as the one's connection to the other. With pervasion (and formulations of pervasion for the purpose of inference), in contrast, with respect merely to the cause successively in a series (e.g., as a series of seed moments in a granary), it is clear that there need be no specification of connection with the cause as the pervader (e.g., seeds thought of in general as producing sprouts). With respect to the pervaded effect, there is specification of connection to the other. In this way, with respect to the pervader (formulated for the purpose of inference, e.g., "Everything that is a sprout has a seed as its cause") whose own nature is (imagined as) both this (e.g., sprout-producer) and not this (e.g., not-a-sprout-producer), there need be no specification of connection to another. In this way, there is no specification of connection with respect to a pervader whose own nature is both this and not this, and there is specification of connection to another with respect to the pervaded, whose nature is this. Through dependence upon what it is to be projected in conceptual construction, there are two ways to understand pervasion (one causally, the other for the purpose of inference).

Comments

The relation between cause and effect goes in two directions. The effect is connected to the cause and the cause is connected to the effect. This connection is specifiable in either or both directions. But when we are making an inference, we generalize and do not specify the unique connection of the effect to its cause. Take as an example smoke and fire. Fire causes smoke and smoke is caused by fire. Fire can thus be inferred from smoke. Although the connection goes in both directions, in inference we ignore the specifics of the causal relationship in order to focus on the generality of pervasion and the cause considered in general as the pervader. Smoke indicates fire, although causally this bit of smoke is, strictly speaking, generated from a union of fire, water, and fuel. We need not detail the specifics of the causal connection to make the inference.

Text and Translation (p. 75, line 27–p. 76, line 1)

> *nanu yadi pūrvāparakālayor ekasvabhāvo bhāvaḥ sarvadā janakatvenājanakatvena vā vyāpta upalabdhaḥ syāt, tadāyaṃ prasaṅgaḥ saṃgacchate. na ca kṣaṇabhaṅgavādinā pūrvāparakālayor ekaḥ kaścid upalabdha iti cet.*

Objection: If one thing with a single nature at both an earlier and later time were experienced as pervaded either by being a producer at all times or a non-producer (at all times), then the bad consequence that you point out (namely, loss of identity) would follow. (But this, what you criticize, is not part of our view.) And (only) for the advocate of destruction in a moment (i.e., only presupposing momentariness) is it not the case that nothing is experienced at (both) an earlier and a later time.

Comments

Ratnakīrti has argued that an enduring thing would either always produce or would never produce. The opponent now objects that Ratnakīrti is begging the question, that he does not accept the false dilemma, that only those so misguided as to presuppose momentariness fail to experience a single thing as the same at an earlier and a later time.

Text and Translation (p. 76, lines 1–5)

> *tad etad atigrāmyam. tathā hi pūrvāparakālayor ekasvabhāvatve satīty asyāyam arthaḥ. parakālabhāvī janako yaḥ svabhāvo bhāvasya sa eva yadi pūrvakālabhāvī, pūrvakālabhāvī vā yo 'janakaḥ svabhāvaḥ sa eva yadi parakālabhāvī tadopalabdham eva jananam ajananaṃ vā syāt. tathā ca sati siddhayor eva svabhāvayor ekatvārope siddham eva jananam ajananaṃ vāsajyata iti.*

Ratnakīrti: The dim-witted would say such—specifically, the meaning of what you said about a single self-nature existing at an earlier and at a later time. If an entity existing at a later time has a producing self-nature that itself exists at an earlier time (too), or if it has a non-producing self-nature at an earlier time that exists at a later time (too), then (in either case) production or non-production would be what was experienced. And that being so, it is shown indeed that, given that its identity is superimposed on what are (now) known to be two self-natures, it is to be adduced that the thing (at one time) is either a producer or a non-producer.

Comments

Ratnakīrti never assumes, in any of the statements in his own voice, that enduring things exist. Here, as elsewhere, he employs a hypothetical syllogism, an indirect argument, to reject the existence of an enduring thing. He has argued that if an enduring thing existed, bad consequences would follow. He now makes clear that the idea of any enduring entity would be the result of a projection of unity upon what are really two distinct entities. Given that an entity at a certain time t_1 produces, if we imagine it as identical to another entity existing at another time t_2 , then we are forced to imagine that the entity at t_1 also produces. The opponent fails to appreciate the hypothetical nature of the argument as well as its adamantine conclusion that nothing can by nature both produce and not produce.

Text and Translation (p. 76, lines 6–9)

> *nanu kāryam eva sahakāriṇam apekṣate, na tu kāryotpattihetuḥ. yasmād dvividhaṃ sāmarthyaṃ nijam āgantukaṃ ca sahakāryantaram, tato 'kṣaṇikasyāpi kramavatsahakārinānātvādapi kramavat kāryanānātvopapatter aśakyaṃ bhāvānāṃ pratikṣaṇam anyānyatvam upapādayitum iti cet.*

Objection: Only the effect depends upon the whole collection of auxiliary causes. In contrast, the cause (*hetu*) that produces is not in this way dependent. Aside from auxiliary causes, there are two kinds of capacity: innate (*nija*) and acquired (*āgantuka*). Your assumption that it is not possible that a non-momentary thing (or anything) have a sequence of effects due to auxiliary causes arriving sequentially makes possible your conclusion that beings are at every moment becoming another and (then yet) another.

Comments

The opponent objects that Ratnakīrti's conclusion that things are momentary depends on the assumption that a sequential appearance of auxiliary causes could not be responsible for a series of effects being produced by a single, enduring cause. This assumption is wrong, the opponent asserts, because there are two kinds of capacity. Innate capacity is not given to a thing by an auxiliary cause; acquired capacity is obtained through an auxiliary. The effect depends upon a whole collection of causal factors. The individual factors can have innate capacity although the effect depends on acquired capacity too. Consequently, a single enduring cause can, over a period of time, acquire a series of capacities from conjunction with a series of different auxiliary causes, and become a factor in the production of a series of different effects.

To count as a "cause" (*hetu*, a non-technical term used by everyone), something need not be in itself sufficient to bring about the effect, although to be an "effect" does presuppose that an entire collection of causal factors has occurred producing it. Of course, the "whole collection" is, from Ratnakīrti's perspective, a non-entity: only particulars exist and have causal power. Our Buddhist proceeds now to target the opponent's mistake in conceiving of the *sāmagrī*, the "whole collection of factors together sufficient," as something real, with causal capacity over and above that of the individual factors that make it up.

Text and Translation (p. 76, lines 9–16)

> *ucyate. bhavatu tāvan nijāgantukabhedena dvividhaṃ sāmarthyam. tathāpi yat prātisvikaṃ vastusvalakṣaṇam arthakriyādharmakam avaśyam abhyupagantavyam, tat kiṃ prāg api paścād eva veti vikalpya yad dūṣaṇam udīritaṃ tatra kim uktam aneneti na pratīmaḥ. yat tu kāryeṇaiva sahakāriṇo 'pekṣyanta ity upaskṛtaṃ tad api nirupayogam. yadi hi kāryam eva svajanmani svatantraṃ syād yuktam etat. kevalam evaṃ sati sahakārisākalyasāmarthyakalpanam aphalam. svatantrād eva hi kāryaṃ kādācit kiṃ bhaviṣyati. tathā ca sati santo hetavaḥ sarvathā 'samarthāḥ. asad etat kāryaṃ svatantram iti viśuddhā buddhiḥ.*

Ratnakīrti: We reply. Let it be supposed, first of all, that there are two kinds of capacity the innate and the acquired. Nevertheless, the self-characterized (*svalakṣaṇa*) individual, which necessarily is to be understood as being causally efficient (i.e., as having capacity), well, is it efficient also at the earlier time or at the later time only? These are the options. We do not comprehend the response that you suppose undermines our argument, (namely) "What is meant by this?"

Objection: Only the effect depends upon auxiliaries. (What is called a cause is not dependent in this way.)

Ratnakīrti: This elaboration is also useless. For, it would be acceptable if the effect could be self-dependent (*svatantra*) in its own coming to be. Only if such were so would the idea that it is the whole collection of auxiliaries that is capable be fruitless. For, sometimes the effect would come to be indeed self-dependently. And when this was the case, the (so-called) causes would in every way be non-capable. The clear understanding (however) is that there is no self-dependent effect.

Comments

Ratnakīrti insists that the distinction between innate and acquired capacity makes no difference to his argument. Something that exists, the individual thing in itself, has the property of capacity necessarily. It has, therefore, innate capacity, and does not acquire capacity from outside. This is the right conception according to arguments presented elsewhere. But whatever elaboration of the idea of what it is to exist an opponent might propose, the fundamental dilemma still faces the advocate of endurance: if things endure, they produce either always or never.

It does not help to add that only an effect has to be dependent upon the whole causal collection to be rightly called an effect, whereas a cause can be something that does not depend upon production actually occurring. Production could, of course, come about only with the help of auxiliaries. If something could be a cause in that sense, something would have to be an effect without those auxiliaries, too, and that would be to say that an effect could arise self-dependently, without sufficient cause. Thus the opponent would create for himself wiggle room only if effects sometimes were self-caused. Self-causation is, however, absurd.

Text and Translation (p. 76, lines 17–20)

> *atha kāryasyaivāyam aparādho yad idaṃ samarthe kāraṇe saty api kadācin nopapadyata iti cet. na tat tarhi tatkāryaṃ svātantryāt. yad bhāṣyam*
>
> > *sarvāvasthāsamāne 'pi kāraṇe yady akāryatā.*
> > *svatantraṃ kāryam evaṃ syān na tatkāryaṃ tathā sati.*

Objection: This anomaly (*aparādha*) belongs only to the effect, which sometimes does not occur even when the cause is capable.

Ratnakīrti: That is wrong. For, the thesis that the effect is self-dependent, is commented on (and refuted in the following verse):

> If there were no effect when there obtained its cause self-same in all situations, then the effect would be self-dependent.
>
> If this were so, it would not be (that there is the causal law, to wit) that given this (i.e., the cause), the effect comes about.

Comments

The opponent has admitted that production of the effect follows upon the whole collection of causal factors, *sāmagrī*. Proper use of the term "cause" is dependent on this conception of the whole collection, he now implies, but anomalous usages are not entirely illegitimate. Specifically, an exception, or "anomaly" (*aparādha*, "transgression") holds with respect to actual effects, such as smoke, about which we say colloquially that fire is its cause even though, properly speaking, only fire in conjunction with wet fuel is the producer. Even though the chief cause, so to say, is present, the effect may not come to be because some auxiliary factor is absent (e.g., water). Although there is such irregularity of common usage, there is no problem, the opponent implies, in saying that such a chief cause is capable of producing the effect, because the idea trades on that of the whole collection of causal factors, *sāmagrī*, which does invariably produce.

Ratnakīrti sees the mistake here as the opponent's holding both (a) the cause endures and (b) there need be no effect despite its presence. He insists that this is inconsistent. If, as (a) implies, the cause is the same in all situations, it cannot produce at one moment and yet not at another. If it did, then the effect would have nothing to do with the cause. This would imply, in turn, that the effect is self-caused—a thesis already rejected as absurd.

The deep problem with the opponent's view is confusion about the notion of a cause. If the cause is the whole collection, *sāmagrī*, then there is no deviation. However, Ratnakīrti has already shown that the individual factors must also be considered producers of the effect in their own right. If the cause is some particular factor (even one we might want to call "the chief cause"), then, on the opponent's view, it follows that the deviation is not just with respect to the effect but with respect to the cause as well. It does not always produce its effect. How then can it be said to have causal capacity? The opponent wants to suggest that it acquires the capacity from auxiliaries, but, in that case, it becomes a distinct entity since it acquires a capacity (a property) that it did not formerly have.

Woo identifies the verse as Prajñākaragupta's: *Pramāṇavārttika-bhāṣya* 3.396.[46]

Text and Translation (p. 76, lines 21–22)

> *atha na tadbhāve bhavatīti tatkāryam ucyate. kiṃ tu tadabhāve na bhavaty eveti vyatirekaprādhānyād iti cet.*

Objection: It is wrong to say that an effect is (defined by the formula) something comes to exist given the existence (of its cause). Rather, it is (defined by the formula) that if it (i.e., the cause) does not exist, then it (the effect) does not come to be: negative correlation (*vyatireka*) is predominant (in definitional projects).

Comments

The opponent disputes Ratnakīrti's definition of causality, contending that the negative formulation he offers is superior to the positive one just given. Thus the aforementioned anomaly occurs because a cause is that which is necessary to an effect, something without which an effect could not be. Thus it is false that whenever there is a cause in this sense its effect occurs. Whenever the cause does not exist, the effect does not exist—this is the right rule.

Clearly, the question is whether a cause, *kāraṇa*, should be considered a necessary or a sufficient condition. The defenders of endurance prefer necessary conditions because a necessary condition need not bring an effect about alone, by itself, as air is necessary but (thankfully) not sufficient for fire. The necessary but insufficient causal factor requires auxiliaries. The defenders of momentariness prefer sufficient conditions because only such things produce immediately. Although Ratnakīrti accepts

---

[46] Woo (1999), p. 209.

that the concept of necessary conditions is important in some contexts, he will insist now, in the next passage, that for the purposes of the argument from causal efficiency—where we are concerned with the innate and essential capacities of things—only sufficient conditions can properly be considered causes.

Text and Translation (p. 76, lines 22–29)

> *na. yadi hi svayaṃ bhavan bhāvayed eva hetuḥ svakāryam, tadā tadabhāvaprayukto 'syābhāva iti pratītiḥ syāt. no ced yathā kāraṇe saty api kāryaṃ svātantryān na bhavati, tathā tadabhāve 'pi svātantryād eva na bhūtam iti śaṅkā kena nivāryeta. yad bhāṣyam*
>
> > *tadbhāve 'pi na bhāvaś ced abhāve 'bhāvitā kutaḥ*
> > *tadabhāvaprayukto 'sya so 'bhāva iti tat kutaḥ.*
>
> *tasmād yathaiva tadabhāve niyamena na bhavati tathaiva tadbhāve niyamena bhaved eva. abhavac ca na tatkāraṇatām ātmanaḥ kṣamate.*

Ratnakīrti: No. For if something existing on its own were a cause just in making its own effect (*svakārya*), then it would be understood that the non-existence of the cause would be connected to the non-existence of the effect. If not, how could the doubt be put to rest that just as the effect does not come to be from its own power although there is a cause (in this sense), so, although there is non-existence of the cause, the effect does not come to be from its own power?

So it is said:

> If though *x* exists there is no coming to be of *y*, then why should it be that *y* does not exist when *x* is absent?
>
> Why is it so, namely, that the very non-existence of this is connected to the non-existence of that?

Therefore, just as only when *x* is non-existent *y* does not exist by rule, in the very same way when *x* exists *y* should indeed come to be by rule. Furthermore, something not existing does not support an attribution of causality to itself.

Comments

The opponent has tried to maintain that a cause can occur without its effect occurring by defining causality as a connection between two types of absence, namely, absence of the cause securing absence of the effect. This would mean, however, that in the case where the cause exists and the effect does not, the effect's non-existence would not be due to the cause's non-existence. The non-existence of the effect would in that case be independent of the cause's presence or absence. This leaves us in doubt about the opposite case where the cause does not exist: is the effect's non-existence due to the non-existence of the putative cause, or, as the other case suggests, is it independent of it? The absence of the cause is only unambiguously and indubitably connected to the absence of the effect if we accept the rule that when the cause exists, the effect occurs too. Then it becomes clear that when the effect does not exist its absence would be due to the absence of the cause. However, on the negative rule alone—without its counterpositive, which takes a positive form (that the presence of the cause guarantees the presence of the effect)—it is possible that the effect be independent of the cause. Thus it would come about on its own—a proposition that is again to be rejected as absurd.

Woo identifies the verse as Prajñākaragupta's: *Pramāṇavārttika-bhāṣya* 1.411.[47]

Text and Translation (p. 77, lines 1–5)

> *yac coktaṃ prathamakāryotpādanakāle hy uttarakāryotpādanasvabhāvaḥ, ataḥ prathamakāla evāśeṣāṇi kāryāṇi kuryād iti. tad idaṃ mātā me vandhyetyādivat svavacanavirodhād ayuktam. yo hy uttarakāryajananasvabhāvaḥ sa katham ādau kāryaṃ kuryāt. na tarhi tatkāryakaraṇasvabhāvaḥ. na hi nilotpādanasvabhāvaḥ pītādikam api karotīti.*

Objection: And what was said (by Ratnakīrti above by way of an objection) is wrong, namely, that a self-nature produces a later effect at the time of producing an earlier effect, that therefore at just that earlier time it would produce all its effects. It is wrong because it contradicts

[47] Woo (1999), p. 210.

itself, like such statements as "My mother is a barren woman." For what has the nature of producing some effect later on, why should it produce that effect in the beginning? It is therefore not the case that it has the nature of producing that (kind of) effect (i.e., a later effect being produced at an earlier time). For it is not the case that something having the nature of producing blue also produces yellow, and so on.

Comments

The opponent, whom Woo identifies as the Nyāya philosopher Bhāsarvajña,[48] now raises another objection against Ratnakīrti's claim that something with a capacity to produce a later effect must produce that effect even at the earlier time. The claim is, the opponent argues, self-contradictory because a later effect, by definition, is produced at a later time. It would be contradictory for a cause to produce the later effect at the earlier time, just as it would be contradictory for something with the capacity to produce something blue also to produce something yellow.

Text and Translation (p. 77, lines 6–12)

> *atrocyate. sthirasvabhāvatve hi bhāvasyottarakālam evedaṃ kāryaṃ na pūrvakālam iti kuta etat. tadabhāvāc ca kāraṇam apy uttarakāryakaraṇasvabhāvam ity api kutaḥ. kiṃ kurmaḥ. uttarakālam eva tasya janmeti cet. astu sthiratve tad anupapadyamānam asthiratām ādiśatu. sthiratve 'py eṣa eva svabhāvas tasya yad uttarakṣaṇa eva karotīti cet. hatedānīṃ pramāṇapratyāśā. dhūmād atrāgnir ity atrāpi svabhāva evāsya yad idānīm atra niragnir api dhūma iti vaktuṃ śakyatvāt.*

Ratnakīrti: To this we reply: why should it be that an effect comes about whose time is later, not one whose time is earlier, given that the self-nature of something endures (i.e., remains constant)? Also, why should it be that, given the absence of it (i.e., of the later effect at the earlier time), the thing still has the self-nature (at the earlier time) of producing at the later time? What do we make of this?

Objection: Its production does not come to be until later—let this stand.

[48] Woo (1999), p. 211.

Ratnakīrti: If it endures, then this is impossible. You should teach non-endurance.

Objection: Given its endurance, its self-nature is just that it produces at a later time.

Ratnakīrti: How now will there be confidence in *pramāṇa*? (For, we say) from (sight of) smoke, "There is fire here," but we could (as easily) say, something's self-nature being just such (as you allege), "Here there is smoke without fire."

Comments

The opponent has proposed indexing effects to time, so that a cause has the capacity to produce a certain effect at a certain time. The later effect obviously cannot be produced at the earlier time. Ratnakīrti counters by asking: Why is it that the cause has the capacity only for producing the later effect and not an earlier version of it? If the selfsame cause endures, it has to have the capacity to produce the earlier version of the effect as well. It also seems strange that we should ascribe the capacity to produce a later effect to a thing that exists at an earlier time, since the later effect is not yet present.

The opponent might try to argue that the later thing does not actually get produced until the later time, but if this were so, Ratnakīrti reasons, then the thing would not have the capacity until the later time, and, consequently, would not be the same entity. If this is the view of the opponent, he might as well teach momentariness, not endurance.

Finally, the opponent might try to argue that the thing now has the self-nature of producing later, but Ratnakīrti points out that this would make inference impossible. The reason we can infer fire from smoke is that there is fire wherever and whenever there is smoke. Fire inferred must have a self-nature productive of the smoke that is visible. If some fire were to have the self-nature of producing later smoke rather than current smoke, then there would be no way to infer a current fire from a current smoke observation.

Text and Translation (p. 77, lines 12–20)

tasmāt pramāṇaprasiddhe svabhāvālambanam. na tu svabhāvālambhanena pramāṇavyālopah. tasmād yadi kāraṇasyottarakāryakārakatvam abhyupagamya kāryasya prathamakṣaṇabhāvitvam āsajyate, syāt svavacanavirodhaḥ. yadi tu kāraṇasya sthiratve kāryasyottarakālatvam evāsaṅgatam ataḥ kāraṇasyāpy uttarakāryajanakatvaṃ vastuto 'saṃbhavi tadā prasaṅgasādhanam idam. jananavyavahāragocaratvaṃ hi jananena vyāptam iti prasādhītam. uttarakāryajananavyavahāragocaratvaṃ ca tvadabhyupagamāt prathamakāryakaraṇakāla eva ghaṭe dharmiṇi siddham. atas tanmātrānubandhina uttarābhimatasya kāryasya prathame kṣaṇe 'saṃbhavād eva prasaṅgaḥ kriyate.

(**Ratnakīrti continues:**) Therefore, there is an objective self-nature in accordance with what is known by way of *pramāṇa*. But this self-nature is not such as would mean the imploding of *pramāṇa*.

Therefore, if accepting that the cause produces the effect later you remain stuck to the view that the effect has to exist at the earlier moment, your very statement is contradictory.

But insofar as only the later existence of the effect is admitted on the assumption that the cause endures—a cause, hence, that (at the earlier time) is productive of the effect at the later time, which is actually impossible—then this is a proof by *prasaṅga*. For, what is shown is that the scope of everyday talk about producing is pervaded by producing.

And that the scope of everyday talk includes, by your account, production at a later time of an effect is shown with respect to a property-bearer, a pot (for example), whose time of producing the effect is the earlier time (a pot, for example, that sports one property, "producing-*x*," before baking and afterwards sports another, "producing-*y*"). Therefore, the unfortunate consequence follows just from the impossibility that your alleged later effect (*y*) is at the earlier moment connected to just that (pot producing-*x*).

Comments

A self-nature that produces is required if anything is to have capacity. If this is denied, then there is no possibility of justification by inference. The advocates of endurance want to say that the thing has the capacity of producing the effect later. They can either say that the effect exists earlier or that it exists later. If they say that the effect exists earlier, they contradict the claim that it is produced only later. But if they say it is only produced at the later time, then the earlier cause produces the later effect. If it endures, however, it must also produce that effect earlier. This is a bad consequence because it is impossible that the earlier thing should both produce and not produce the later effect.

All of this just confirms that anything appropriately called a producer must produce at that time. The opponent wants to include producing an effect later in the scope of production talk, but if it is called a producer at the earlier time it must produce at that time. Being a producer at the earlier moment of an effect that only comes about later is impossible, because it just is not a producer at that time.

The example of the pot is common across schools of philosophy. According to the realist opponent we presume is being addressed, colors are effects, in a sense, of things that are colored, as a pot can be colored red or black. According to Ratnakīrti, a red pot is patently not the same thing as a black pot; the colors are different. No red pot is black. But that no producer is a non-producer runs deeper than this, beyond color and unessential properties to the core of what anything is. Ratnakīrti makes the point explicitly in what comes next.

Text and Translation (p. 77, lines 20–22)

> *na hi nīlakārake 'pi pītakārakatvārope pītasaṃbhāvaprasaṅgaḥ svavacanavirodho nāma. tad evaṃ śaktaḥ sahakāryanapekṣitatvād jananena vyāptaḥ. ajanayaṃś*[49] *ca śaktāśaktatvaviruddhadharmādhyāsād bhinna eva.*

(Ratnakīrti continues:) For, this is not the problem of the possibility of yellow, where it is imagined that something that produces blue also produces yellow. Patently, your very statement is contradictory. Something capable is pervaded by producing because it is not dependent on auxiliary causes. The non-producer is absolutely distinct (from the producer) because of the imposition of contrary (*viruddha*) properties, (namely) being capable and not being capable.

Comments

This is not the kind of mistake we find in the case of imposing the notion of producing-yellow on something that produces blue. There may

---

[49] Reading *ajanayaṃś* instead of *ajanaryaṃś*.

be wiggle room for the opponent in that conception, though we philosophers of momentariness believe that nothing blue could be the same entity as something yellow. In such a case, one mistakenly imagines that the blue-producer also produces yellow. This is not contradiction. The opponent, in contrast, has made a genuinely contradictory claim. Ratnakīrti has shown that a capable thing does not depend upon auxiliary causes and that it produces. The opponent has asserted that the seed that is not producing is capable, but a seed that is not producing is not capable. The opponent thus imagines that the seed is both capable and incapable. These are genuinely contrary (*viruddha*) properties.

Text and Translation (p. 77, line 23–p. 78, line 4)

> *nanu bhavatu prasaṅgaviparyayabalād ekakāryaṃ prati śaktāsaktatvalakṣaṇaviruddhadharmādhyāsaḥ. tathāpi na tato bhedaḥ sidhyati. tathā hi bījam aṅkurādikaṃ kurvad yadi yenaiva svabhāvenāṅkurādikaṃ karoti tenaiva kṣityādikaṃ tadā kṣityādīnām apy aṅkurasvābhāvyāpattiḥ. nānāsvabhāvatvena tu kārakatve svabhāvānām anyonyābhāvāvyabhicāritvād ekatra bhāvābhāvau parasparaviruddhau syātām ity ekam api bījaṃ bhidyeta. evaṃ pradīpo 'pi tailakṣayavarttidāhādikam. tathā pūrvarūpam apy uttararūparasagandhādikam anekaiḥ[50] svabhāvaiḥ parikalitaṃ karoti. teṣāṃ ca svabhāvānām anyonyābhāvāvyabhicārād viruddhānāṃ yoge pradīpādikaṃ bhidyeta. na ca bhidyate. tan na viruddhadharmādhyāso bhedakaḥ. tathā bījasyāṅkuraṃ prati kārakatvaṃ gardabhādikaṃ praty akārakatvam iti kārakatvākārakatve 'pi viruddhau dharmau. na ca tadyoge 'pi bīja-bhedaḥ. tad evam ekatra bīje pradīpe rūpe ca vipakṣe paridṛśyamānaḥ śaktāsaktatvādir viruddhadharmādhyāso na ghaṭāder bhedaka iti.*

Objection: (No.) Let it be granted that by the force of a transformed *prasaṅga* there is imposition of contrary properties of such a kind as capacity and non-capacity with respect to a single effect. Even so, no distinctness is thereby established. There is, for example, a seed that produces a sprout and so on. If one and the same self-nature producing a sprout and

[50] Reading *anekaiḥ* instead of *anaikaiḥ*.

so on produces the (necessary) soil and so on, then the soil and so on would be implicated in the nature of the sprout (which is absurd). But on the assumption that the thing is a producer (on our account) by virtue of various self-natures, existence (of producing-*x*) and non-existence (of producing-*x*), which are mutually opposed because of the non-deviation of the mutual absence of their self-natures, would be in one place. Thus a single seed would be split (into many). Thus, a lamp should include the burning of the wick and the consuming of the oil. In this way, the earlier form produces an effect including color, taste, smell, and so on, by (as you allege) "multiple self-natures." And because of the non-deviation of the mutual absence of those self-natures, which are opposites, the lamp, etc., would be split. But they are not split. (The lamp and the seed are single entities that endure.)

Therefore, attribution of contrary properties is not a differentiator. The seed is a producer of the sprout, but a non-producer of an ass and so on. Therefore, producerhood and non-producerhood are also contrary properties. And it is not the case that the seed is divided, although there is a joining (of those "opposites" in the seed). Therefore in this way with respect to a single thing—e.g., a seed, a lamp, color—the imposition of contrary qualities beheld, (namely) capacity and non-capacity, is not a distinguisher of such things as the pot (which is, for example, one and the same before and after baking).

Comments

The opponent concedes that Ratnakīrti has shown that contrary properties are being imposed upon a single entity through his *prasaṅga* argument. Ratnakīrti has drawn the conclusion from this that the earlier entity must be distinct from the later entity. The opponent now argues that despite the fact that the seed is being depicted as having contrary properties, this does not prove that the earlier and later seeds are not the same entity.

This is only a slight expansion of the idea, which is patently correct, that a seed that has the capacity to produce a banana tree does not produce a donkey. Such an entity in virtue of having not just incompatible but contrary properties would be shown to be a group of distinct entities according to Ratnakīrti's argument. The same would be true of the lamp, which produces many effects simultaneously such as consumption of fuel, burning of the wick, and production of light. All of these distinct capacities should demonstrate that the lamp is really distinct from itself even at a single moment. But it is one and the same lamp in fact. These various capacities cannot occur in a single entity, according to the Buddhist, because one is always absent where the other is present. But this leads to the conclusion that even a lamp would be divided into a group. The lamp is in fact a single thing with multiple capacities. The seed is in fact a single thing both capable and incapable. Thus there is no reason to conclude that just because there are contrary properties, a thing is really divided into several distinct things.

Text and Translation (p. 78, lines 5–15)

> *atra brūmaḥ. bhavatu tāvad bījādīnām anekakāryakāritvād dharmabhūtānekasvabhāvabhedaḥ, tathāpi kaḥ prastāvo viruddhadharmādhyāsasya. svabhāvānāṃ hy anyonyābhavāvyabhicāre bhedaḥ prāptāvasaro na virodhaḥ. virodhas tu yadvidhāne yanniṣedho yanniṣedhe ca yadvidhānaṃ tayor ekatra dharmiṇi parasparaparihārasthitatayā syāt. tad atraikaḥ svabhāvaḥ svābhāvena viruddho yukto bhāvābhāvavat. na tu svabhāvāntareṇa ghaṭatvavastutvavat. evam aṅkurādikāritvam tadakāritvena viruddham na punar vastvantarakāritvena. pratyakṣavyāpāraś cātra yathā nānādharmair adhyāsitaṃ bhāvam abhinnaṃ vyavasthāpayati tathā tatkāryakārinaṃ kāryāntarakāriṇaṃ ca. tad yadi pratiyogitvābhāvād anyonyābhāvāvyabhicāriṇāv api svabhāvāv aviruddhau tadkārakatvānyākārakatve vā viṣayabhedād aviruddhe. tat kim āyātam ekakāryaṃ prati śaktāśaktatvayoḥ parasparapratiyoginor viruddhayor dharmayoḥ. etayor api punar avirodhe virodho nāma dattajalāñjaliḥ.*

Ratnakīrti: To this we answer. Let it be granted, first of all, that because seeds, etc., are producers of more than one effect, there is more than one distinct self-nature which is a property (or property-entity, *dharma*). Nevertheless, (let us ask) what is the occasion for imposition of contrary properties? For, given that the mutual absences of (two) self-natures (*x* and *y*) do not deviate, the distinctness (of *x* from *y* and vice-versa), which is a patent fact, is not a contradiction (*virodha*).

However, here is a contradiction: to deny something while that same thing is being asserted, or to assert something while that same thing is being denied, such that (to use your realist terminology) the two would be mutually exclusive, with respect to a single property-bearer.

Therefore, in such a case (only) would it be appropriate to say that a single self-nature would be contrary to its self-nature, like existence and non-existence. But with another self-nature this is not the case, like being-a-pot and being-a-thing.

In this way, production of the sprout, etc., is contrary to (*viruddha*) non-production of it, but it is not contrary to the production of another (effect). And what perception shows here, well, inasmuch as it establishes (as you say) a non-split being on which various properties are imposed; so it establishes it as producing this effect and not producing some other effect. Therefore, if because of a lack of (explicit) contraposition two self-natures are not opposed although they do not deviate in being in the relationship of mutual absence (mutual exclusion); or, if the two, production of something and non-production of something else, because of the difference of scope (*viṣaya*), are not contrary (although there is likewise non-deviation in their mutual absences); then indeed how could it be that two properties, capacity and incapacity, which stand mutually as the absentee to the other, could be contrary (*viruddha*)? If these two are not contrary, (the concept of) contrariety itself would receive the (death knell, the death rites of the) hollow palm filled with water (*jalāñjali*).

Comments

Ratnakīrti begins his response by granting for the sake of argument the realist terminology of property-bearers and properties and the idea that there can be multiple self-natures present in a single thing like a lamp that has many distinct capacities. For the Buddhist, the right view is that even at a single moment, something like a lamp is really a collection of different property-entities. However, in the examples cited by the opponent there is no putting together of contrary (*viruddha*) properties. The lamp may produce the consumption of fuel and the burning of the wick and the generation of light, but these are not contrary properties. They can be included in the same collection. Something is contradictory when the very thing being asserted is also denied. We do not need to deny that the lamp consumes fuel to assert that it also burns the wick. This is like the case of pothood and thinghood: something can be a pot and also a thing. Capacity and incapacity, however, are like existence and non-existence: these cannot occur in the same entity—to talk the talk of the realists—

because they are mutually exclusive. Wherever the one is, the other is not. Given this, an entity like a seed cannot be the bearer of two such properties. If the opponent tries to deny that these are truly opposed properties, then it is not clear what we could mean by "contradiction" (*viruddhatā*) or contrariety. It would be the death of the very notion.

Text and Translation (p. 78, lines 16–19)

> *bhavatu tarhy ekakāryāpekṣayaiva sāmarthyāsāmarthyayor virodhaḥ. kevalaṃ yathā tad eva kāryaṃ prati kvacid deśe śaktir deśāntare cāśaktir iti deśabhedād aviruddhe śaktyaśaktī tathaikatraiva kāryakālabhedād apy aviruddhe. yathā pūrvaṃ niṣkriyaḥ sphaṭikaḥ sa eva paścāt sakriya iti cet.*

Objection: Then let it stand that there is opposition (*virodha*) between capacity and non-capacity precisely with respect to a single effect. However, just as capacity and non-capacity are not contrary given a difference of place—capacity for a certain effect when the thing is in one place and incapacity (for that effect) when it is in another place—so, even with respect to a single thing, capacity and non-capacity need not be contrary because of difference of the time of the effect—as a crystal can be a cause (of some particular effect) earlier (when, e.g., a rose is laid behind it) and later not a cause (of that effect, when, e.g., the rose is picked up).

Comments

The opponent, whom Woo again identifies as Bhāsarvajña,[51] concedes that Ratnakīrti has shown that there is opposition (*virodha*) between capacity and non-capacity with respect to the same effect at the same place and time, but objects that there is no opposition between capacity and non-capacity with respect to the same effect at different places or at different times. There is an analogy between spatial and temporal difference. In the spatial case, we all agree without contradiction that something can have the capacity to produce an effect in a certain place and non-capacity to produce that effect in another place. For instance, a certain seed has the capacity to produce a sprout at the place in the field where it is planted, but does not have the capacity to produce the sprout in the granary.

---

[51] Woo (1999), p. 223.

In the same way, the opponent argues, one and the same entity can have the capacity to produce the effect at one time and not have that capacity at another time: this is not a contradiction. A crystal looks red when a rose is placed behind it, but does not sport that appearance when the rose is taken away.

Text and Translation (p. 78, lines 19–22)

> *ucyate. na hi vayaṃ paribhāṣāmātrād ekatra kārye deśabhedād aviruddhe śaktyaśaktī brūmaḥ, kiṃ tu virodhābhāvāt. taddeśakāryakāritvaṃ hi taddeśakāryākāritvena viruddham. na punar deśāntare tatkāryākāritvena vā.*

Ratnakīrti: We answer. We do not say that capacity and non-capacity are unopposed (in the case of different places) just because of some technical rule (*paribhāṣā*) due to difference of place with respect to the effect, but because there is no opposition. For, being a producer with respect to the effect in a place is opposed to being a non-producer with respect to that effect in that place. But there is no opposition to not producing that effect in another place, nor to being the producer of another effect.

Comments

Ratnakīrti rejects the analogy between space and time. He argues that we must decide in each case whether there is opposition. We cannot just formulate a technical rule that difference of place renders capacity and non-capacity compatible and then apply that rule to temporal difference. We must determine whether opposition arises in each case. Unstated is the assumption that it is acceptable to all sides that perceptually established correlations can show mutual absence and thus opposition, and that no one has perceived capacity and non-capacity for the same effect together in the one and the same cause. In the case of capacity and non-capacity in different places, no opposition occurs, but there is opposition between capacity and non-capacity in the same place.

Text and Translation (p. 78, lines 23–25)

> *yady evaṃ tatkālakāryakāritvaṃ tatkālakāryākāritvena viruddham. na punaḥ kālāntare*

tatkāryākāritvenānyakāryakāritvena vā. tat kathaṃ kālabhede 'pi virodha iti cet.

Objection: Then if something is the producer of an effect at a certain time, there is opposition with being a non-producer of that effect at that time, but there is no opposition with being a non-producer of the effect at another time nor with being the producer of another effect. How, then, is there opposition (between capacity and non-capacity) even when the times are distinct?

Comments

The opponent retorts that the same reasoning can apply to temporal difference. When something is capable of producing an effect at a certain time, there is no opposition with its being incapable of producing that effect at another time. It is true, of course, that it cannot have both capacity and incapacity with respect to the same effect at the same time. But just as capacity and incapacity cannot occur in the same place but can occur in different places, so they cannot occur at the same time but can occur when the times are different.

Text and Translation (p. 78, line 25–p. 79, line 2)

ucyate. dvayor hi dharmayor ekatra dharmiṇy anavasthitiniyamaḥ parasparaparihārasthitilakṣaṇo virodhaḥ. sa ca sākṣātparasparapratyanīkatayā bhāvābhāvavad vā bhavet, ekasya vā niyamena pramāṇāntareṇa bādhanān nityatvasattvavad vā bhaved iti na kaścid arthabhedaḥ. tad atraikadharmiṇi tatkālatatkāryakāritvādhāre kālāntare tatkāryākāritvasyānyakāryakāritvasya vā niyamena pramāṇāntareṇa bādhanād virodhaḥ. tathā hi yatraiva dharmiṇi tatkālakāryakāritvam upalabdhaṃ na tatraiva kālāntare tatkāryākāritvam anyakāryakāritvaṃ vā brahmaṇāpy upasaṃhartum śakyate, yenānayor avirodhaḥ syāt. kṣaṇāntare kathitaprasaṅgaviparyayahetubhyām avaśyaṃbhāvena dharmibhedaprasādhanāt.

Ratnakīrti: We answer. Opposition is defined by a state of mutual avoidance, whose rule is the non-presence (*anavasthiti*) of two (contrary) properties in a single property-bearer. Or, opposition may be taken to be like existence and non-existence, which are in immediate contrariety (*pratyanīkatā*). Or, opposition may be taken to be like the permanence and the existence of one and the same thing because of the blocking (of the one by the other and vice-versa) as is shown by the rule (that they do not occur together), that is to say, as is shown by another *pramāṇa*. There is no difference in meaning (in these cases).

Therefore, in the case at issue where we are supposing a single property-bearer as the support or locus (*ādhāra*) of production of a certain effect at a certain time, there is opposition—because of the blocking, as is shown by the rule (of mutual absence, that is to say, as is shown by another *pramāṇa*—with its producing that effect at another time or with producing a different effect. In the case at issue, just where the production of a certain effect at a certain time is experienced, not even Brahman (the Absolute) has the power to assert, to add, or make it so (*upasaṃhartum*), that just there with the very same property-bearer but at another time there is this production or that there is no production at this time or production of a different effect, such that there would be no opposition between the two. It is proved that there is necessarily a distinct property-bearer at another moment, by means of a *prasaṅga* and its transformation, which have been given above.

Comments

Ratnakīrti gives a working account of opposition, and while admitting that no opposition arises between capacity in one place and incapacity in another, insists that opposition does occur between capacity and incapacity at different times. Something that is a producer of a certain effect at a certain time does not produce that very same effect at a different time. To accommodate his opponent's perspective, Ratnakīrti relies on an understanding of opposition as a relation between two properties such that they cannot occur in the same property-bearer. This relation is exemplified (everyone agrees) by existence and non-existence: wherever one occurs, the other does not occur. The relation also exists, he reminds us, in the case under discussion. The defender of enduring entities wants to say that existence and non-momentariness occur in the same property-bearer, but this is ruled out by *pramāṇa*, as Ratnakīrti has argued all along. It is ruled out by a *prasaṅga* and its transformation.

Thus it is supposed, perhaps counterintuitively, that capacity at one time and non-capacity at another can be mutually opposed. But this statement is vague. Granting for the sake of argument that a single property-bearer can exist at different moments, if we propose that it has capacity to produce at one time and non-capacity at another, we must mean different effects. If we are talking about capacity for one and the same effect, these do not occur together. Consult perception if you have doubt about this.

Thus we should not ascribe to a single property-bearer properties that are experienced as mutually absent. We see something produce an effect at a certain time. Even if we assume that it is the same property-bearer at another time, still it could not be a non-producer of that same effect at whatever time. A single property-bearer at a single time may be considered to have capacity and non-capacity for *x* with respect to different places or with respect to a different effect *y* without any opposition. We find positive examples of this such as a seed's producing a sprout in one place but not in others. Of course, in the case of temporal difference, the examples are disputed. Buddhists hold that there is a positive example of mutual opposition between capacity and incapacity despite difference in time. Ratnakīrti's main move in the passage at hand is to show that the burden of proof belongs to the opponent to establish that a single property-bearer endures over time. Only thus would there be support for the claim that temporal difference renders capacity and incapacity for one and the same effect compatible with respect to a single property-bearer. Unless this can be done on independent grounds, the objection cannot undermine the Buddhist argument.

Text and Translation (p. 79, line 3–10)

> *na ca pratyabhijñānād ekatvasiddhaḥ, tatpauruṣasya nirmūlitatvāt. ata eva vajro 'pi pakṣakukṣau nikṣiptaḥ. katham asau sphaṭiko varākaḥ kālabhedenābhedaprasādhanāya dṛṣṭāntībhavitum arhati. na caivam samānakālakāryāṇāṃ deśabhede 'pi dharmibhedo yukto bhedaprasādhakapramāṇābhāvāt. indriyapratyakṣeṇa nirastavibhramāśaṅkenābhedaprasādhanāc ceti na kālabhede 'pi śaktyaśaktyor virodhaḥ svasamayamātrād apahastayituṃ śakyaḥ, samayapramāṇayor apravṛtter iti. tasmāt sarvatra viruddhadharmādhyāsasiddhir eva bhedasiddhiḥ. vipratipannaṃ prati tu viruddhadharmādhyāsād bhedavyavahāraḥ sādhyate.*

(Ratnakīrti continues:) It is not the case, furthermore, that unity (over time) is established by (so-called) recognition (e.g., "This is that Devadatta I saw previously"), because there is no foundation of the idea that it is the same person (from one time to the next). Therefore, even the diamond (which seems to endure unchanging) is excluded (as an example) inasmuch as it falls within the cases at issue. How, then, is it that a lowly crystal can show non-distinctness through different times?

And it is not the case that in this way it is appropriate to say that because there is no *pramāṇa* proving difference (over time) there are (nevertheless) distinct property-bearers because effects at the same time have distinct places, or that it is proved by sense perception, where suspicion of error is eliminated, that there is no difference (over time). The opposition between capacity and non-capacity cannot be thrown out on the presumption that they pertain to distinct times, because there is only the thing's own occasion (*sva-samaya*). For neither *pramāṇa* nor occasions extend (past the occasion of any individual case).

Therefore, in all cases, to show that contrary properties have been imputed is to prove difference. With respect to the disputed issue, ordinary speech presupposing difference proceeds from imposition of contrary properties.

Comments

Ratnakīrti now anticipates an attempt by the opponent to establish the unity of the property-bearer through time by means of an argument from recognition (*pratyabhijñāna*). We often have cognitions such as "This is the same Devadatta I saw yesterday." The opponent might try to argue that such cognitions would not be possible unless Devadatta were the same property-bearer seen at the earlier time. But Ratnakīrti points out there is no basis for regarding Devadatta as the same property-bearer through time. It is at issue whether or not Devadatta is a single property-bearer enduring through time.

Note that such cognitions sometimes occur even when everyone would agree it is not the same property-bearer. We think we recognize Devadatta from across the room, but on closer inspection we discover that it is someone else. This suggests that recognition can be falsely induced. Thus a single property-bearer cannot be inferred from the occurrence of recognition. This is true also of the diamond, which is very hard to destroy. The question of whether it endures is at issue as well, and so the lowly crystal—mentioned as something that can be changed easily (easily broken and chipped, whereas a diamond is famously adamantine)—is also at issue and may not be assumed to be an example of an enduring property-bearer with capacity at one moment and incapacity at another.

With respect to spatial difference, the opponent admits difference of property-bearers. Temporal difference cannot be held out as anomalous. Perception is itself restricted to its own moment. Perception informed by remembering shows just the opposite of the opponent's contention, namely, that there is change. The opponent thus has no argument that one and the same thing can have both capacity and incapacity for an effect on different occasions. A thing has only its own occasion, and a difference in properties—especially an imputation of contrary properties, which are defined as properties that cannot occur together—proves that there are different things, e.g., Devadatta seen yesterday and a different entity, conveniently called by the same name, Devadatta seen today. Even in everyday speech, we recognize differences once we have become apprised of opposition.

In sum, the opponent has no available example to support the claim that capacity for an effect at one time is not contrary to incapacity for the effect at another.

Text and Translation (p. 79, lines 11–13)

> *nanu tathāpi sattvam idam anaikāntikam evāsādhāraṇatvāt sandigdhavyatirekitvād vā. yathā hīdaṃ kramākramanivṛttāv akṣaṇikān nivṛttaṃ tathā sāpekṣatvānapekṣatvayor ekatvānekatvayor api vyāpakayor nivṛttau kṣaṇikād api.*

Objection: In the very same way, this (your prover) existence is nothing but inconclusive, because there is no example of a positive correlation (outside of the cases at issue). Alternatively, it is inconclusive, because the negative form of pervasion is dubious (given that examples of negative correlations would have to be non-existent). For, just as something would be excluded (as you claim) from non-momentariness (that is to say, would be momentary) because it is excluded from successive or non-successive production, in that same way, because it is momentary it would fall outside even the pervaders, dependence/independence and unity/multiplicity. (And nothing is neither dependent on another nor independent, and neither a unity nor a composite of many.)

Comments

This passage is the beginning of a long *pūrvapakṣa* where the opponent, whom Woo identifies as Vācaspati Miśra,[52] charges that if Ratnakīrti's reasoning is correct, then it follows that his own prover, existence, is inconclusive. Ratnakīrti's argument is that something non-momentary cannot have causal efficiency either successively or non-successively. The opponent counters that if one and the same thing cannot at different times have capacity and incapacity, by the same token a momentary thing could be neither dependent nor independent (*apekṣatva-anapekṣatva*) and neither one nor many (*ekatva-anekatva*). Since each of these pairs is exhaustive of everything that exists, to show that a momentary thing can be neither amounts to showing that no such thing exists.

This would render Ratnakīrti's inference inconclusive in two ways. First, given that momentary things do not exist, there would be no undisputed positive correlations supporting the purported pervasion between existence and momentariness. Second, if the pervasion is to be supported only by negative correlations (*vyatireka*), all of the examples would have to be non-existent, and therefore unavailable as evidence. Consequently, the desired negative correlation would also remain dubious.

Text and Translation (p. 79, lines 13–24)

> *tathā hy upasarpaṇapratyayena devadattakarapallavādinā sahacaro bījakṣaṇaḥ pūrvasmād eva puñjāt samartho jāto 'napekṣa ādyātiśayasya janaka iṣyate. tatra ca samānakuśūlajanmasu bahuṣu bījasantāneṣu kasmāt kiñcid eva bījaṃ paramparayā 'ṅkurotpādānuguṇam upajanayati bījakṣaṇaṃ nānye bījakṣaṇā bhinnasantānāntaḥpātinaḥ. na hy upasarpaṇapratyayāt prāg eva teṣāṃ samānāsamānasantānavartināṃ bījakṣaṇānāṃ kaścit paramparātiśayaḥ. athopasarpaṇapratyayāt prāṅ na tatsantānavartino 'pi janayanti, paramparayāpy aṅkurotpādānuguṇaṃ bījakṣaṇaṃ bījamātrajananāt teṣām. kasyacid eva bījakṣaṇasyopasarpaṇapratyayasahabhūva ādyātiśayotpādaḥ. hanta tarhi tadabhāve saty utpanno 'pi na*

---

[52] Woo (1999), p. 229.

janayed eva. tathā ca kevalānāṃ vyabhicārasaṃbhavād ādyātiśayotpādakam aṅkuraṃ vā prati kṣityādīnāṃ parasparāpekṣāṇām evotpādakatvam akāmenāpi svīkartavyam. ato na tāvad anapekṣā kṣaṇikasya saṃbhavinī.

(Objector 1 continues:) For example, a seed-moment (as you would say), born at quite an earlier moment from a heap (of conditions) as capable (of producing a sprout) when helped along by gathering conditions (*upasarpaṇa-pratyaya*) such as Devadatta's hands and fingers, is desired (by you) to be the independent generator of a first additional capacity (*ādya-atiśaya*, i.e., a capacity a final seed-moment has for a succeeding sprout-moment). Given that there are many seed-series, all born in the same granary, why, with respect to this (change in generating such capacity), does just some one particular seed, through a sequence, give rise to the seed-moment with suitable properties to produce a sprout? Why not other seed-moments which fall within distinct series? For, it is not the case that prior to the gathering conditions (being all in place) there is any additional capacity coming about through a sequence from seed-moments existing in the same or in different series.

Objection (by objector 2 to objector 1): Prior to the gathering conditions, those seed-moments, though they occur in the same series, do not produce; they do not produce a seed-moment fit to produce a sprout, because they produce only a seed. Just one particular seed (that is to say, seed-series) gets helped out by the gathering conditions (Devadatta's fingers, soil, water, etc.) such that production of a first additional capacity (for subsequent sprout-moments) occurs.

Reply (by objector 1): Look here! In that case, if there is no help from (still further) gathering conditions, an additional capacity, though produced, would itself not produce (a sprout).

And in this way, because of the possibility of deviation about which moments themselves produce a first additional capacity, or produce a sprout, it is to be accepted against your will that (auxiliary conditions such as) soil and the like, which are indeed (not independent but) mutually dependent (in producing the sprout), are themselves producers (though none by itself sufficient to produce a sprout). Therefore, no such independence (of production) as you desire on the part of the momentary is possible.

Comments

The opponent begins by attempting to show that a momentary thing cannot be independently a producer of anything. According to the doctrine of momentariness, we should conceive of a seed as a series of seed-moments, the last of which gives rise to a first sprout-moment in a series of sprout-moments. Some seed-moments in a series encounter various auxiliary conditions which may arrive sequentially. One seed-moment is grasped by Devadatta's hand, another is placed in the earth, another encounters water, and so on. Each of these produces another seed-moment, but each encounter with a gathering condition makes a subsequent seed-moment slightly different and progressively closer to being capable of independently producing a sprout. Eventually there arises a seed-moment that encounters the final condition necessary to produce a seed-moment that is independently capable, that is to say, that has a new type of capacity, a capacity for sprout-production. So, from a certain perspective, it is a heap of conditions, including an immediately prior seed-moment, that collectively gives rise to a final seed-moment fit to produce a sprout. Such a final seed-moment does not need anything else to produce the sprout; it is independently capable. The final seed-moment has an absolutely new capacity and gives rise to a first sprout-moment. The new thing produced is no longer another seed-moment; it is a sprout-moment. And where the seed-moment has a tendency to produce another seed-moment unless acted upon by something else, a sprout-moment has different reproductive power: it produces another sprout-moment, which in turn also tends to produce yet another sprout moment.

The opponent now argues that on this picture there is a serious problem of ambiguity concerning what is produced. Where does the seed-series end and the sprout-series begin? If the final seed-moment with its new and additional capacity is considered to act independently at the time of the production of the first sprout-moment, then it should produce another seed-moment like itself, not a sprout!

In the granary, there are many seed-series, not all of which give rise to sprouts. Only seed-series where the appropriate gathering conditions are encountered in sequence terminate in a seed-moment that produces the first in a series of sprout-moments. Before the gathering conditions are encountered, none of the seed-moments in the granary can give rise to the seed-moment that has the first additional capacity, that is to say, none of them can produce a seed-moment that is independently capable of producing that new power. In the absence of gathering conditions, each seed-moment will give rise to another seed-moment like itself. So why should the seed-moment that has the additional capacity not also give rise to a seed-moment like itself and not a sprout?

On Ratnakīrti's conception, once the gathering conditions have all come in sequence, there is no reason not to expect that the first sprout-moment should arise immediately. However, there has to be a final seed-moment that is the first to have sprout-production capacity. But if this is an independently capable seed-moment, then we render the auxiliary conditions otiose. But if no auxiliary condition is required, then there is no reason why there should not be continuation of the seed series. How, then, will there be production of the first sprout-moment? There is an inconsistency between positing such an independently acting seed-moment and acknowledging the causal role of auxiliary factors.

It might be argued that just as the final seed-moment is independently capable due to interaction with the final earth-moment (and other factors), in that way the final earth-moment is also independently capable of producing the sprout or at least the seed-moment that has the new additional power (as are all the final moments in all the series of the various factors). The problem with this is that the auxiliary factors and the final seed-moment are dependent on one another when they act to produce the sprout. Otherwise, it must be admitted that the auxiliary factors are not needed for the production of the sprout.

It makes no sense, therefore, to regard a final seed-moment as independently capable of producing a sprout-series. Without a further auxiliary, a seed-moment, however pregnant with additional capacity through its predecessors having encountered gathering conditions, would produce only another seed-moment, not a sprout. There is thus no explanation why a sprout should be produced.

Text and Translation (p. 79, lines 24–28)

> *nāpy apekṣā yujyate, samasamayakṣaṇayoḥ savyetaragoviṣāṇayor ivopakāryopakārakabhāvāyogād iti nāsiddhaḥ prathamo vyāpakābhāvaḥ. api cāntyo bījakṣaṇo 'napekṣā 'ṅkurādikaṃ kurvan yadi yenaiva rūpeṇāṅkuraṃ karoti tenaiva kṣityādikaṃ*

tadā kṣityādinām apy aṅkurasvābhāvyāpattir abhinnakāraṇatvād iti na tāvad ekatvasaṃbhavaḥ

(Objector 1 continues:) Nor is dependence (of the two options in the first dilemma destructive of your view) any good (that is to say, nothing momentary could be a producer in depending on other causal factors), because two moments at the same time, which would be like the left and right horns of a cow, cannot stand in a helper-helped relationship. Therefore, the absence of the first pair of pervaders (dependence/independence as opposed to unity/multiplicity) is not (contrary to your claim) unestablished (for things allegedly momentary: nothing is momentary since everything is a producer either dependently or independently).

Furthermore, if the last seed-moment produces the sprout independently, such that in whatever way it produces the sprout in that same way (each of the auxiliary conditions) soil and the like produce it, then there is the unfortunate consequence that (the auxiliary conditions) soil and the like also have the self-nature (of producing) a sprout, because the causality would be identical. There is, then, no possibility of unity (of a momentary thing as a cause, since it would have to comprise soil, etc., all the auxiliary conditions).

Comments

The opponent now argues that it makes no sense to think of the final seed-moment as acting in dependence upon the auxiliary conditions. The final seed-moment is a momentary entity. A momentary entity cannot be acted upon by another momentary entity because there is no time for interaction. By the time the auxiliary factor provided assistance to a particular seed-moment, that seed-moment would no longer exist. The only option seems to be to go back to the view that each of the auxiliary factors acts independently, each being the result of a conjunction of factors in the previous moment. But it has already been argued that this model cannot capture the supportive role of the auxiliary factors at the moment of production. Here the opponent suggests another problem: if each of the factors acts independently, then each should produce its own sprout, independently of the others. There would then be many sprouts produced and not just one, which is absurd. Or if there is to be only one sprout, the last "seed"-moment would have to comprise soil and the like and thus that moment would not be a unity.

Text and Translation (p. 79, line 29–p. 80, line 3)

> *nanu rūpāntareṇa karoti. tathā hi bījasyāṅkuraṃ praty upādānatvam. kṣityādikaṃ tu prati sahakāritvam. yady evaṃ sahakāritvopādānatve kim ekaṃ tattvaṃ nānā vā. ekaṃ cet kathaṃ rūpāntareṇa janakam. nānātve tv anayor bījād bhedo 'bhedaḥ vā. bhede kathaṃ bījasya janakatvaṃ tābhyām evāṅkurādīnām utpatteḥ. abhede vā kathaṃ bījasya na nānātvaṃ bhinnatādātmyāt, etayor vaikatvam ekatādātmyāt.*

Objection (by objector 2 to objector 1): (No, it is a unity.) It produces with another nature. For example, the seed is the main cause with respect to the sprout. But with respect to soil (considered as the main cause) or the like, the seed is an auxiliary.

Reply (by objector 1): If this were so, then with respect to the main cause and the auxiliary causes, is there one (causal) principle or many? If there is one, how then is there (as you claim) production along with another nature?

But if there are many (causal principles), are these two (the main cause and the auxiliary causes) different or non-different from the seed? If they are different, how is the seed a producer, since production of the sprout is only from those two (the main cause and the auxiliaries)? Or if they are not different, how is the seed not multiple, because its identity is split, or else those two are one, because they have a single identity?

Comments

The opponent considers an objection to the argument that the momentary thing cannot produce dependently. It produces because it has a special nature provided by auxiliary causes. Or, the "with another nature" in the text could mean simply that the last seed-moment produces *along with* auxiliaries. In any case, we regard the seed as the main cause (*upādāna*) because it is the continuing material series that leads into the sprout series. But we do not want to ignore the supporting role of the other factors. They allow the last seed-moment to produce by giving it a special nature, or by aiding the production of the special nature, such that it does produce dependently, requiring the auxiliary factors. That is to say, soil and the like are auxiliaries whatever the precise relationship. Being an auxiliary and being the main cause are correlative notions. If you wish to focus on the causal role of the soil, then it is fine to say that soil is the main cause and the seed an auxiliary.

The issue is the role of auxiliary causes at the moment of production. The opponent has argued that they can have no role at that moment because they do not exist long enough to interact with one another. Ratnakīrti has suggested that the seed-moment produces because it has a special nature, or altered productivity, when in the presence of the auxiliaries. It does therefore produce dependently. (Below, he makes explicit his view that the moment, though singular as a cause, has multiple effects. This makes room for auxiliary causality in that soil, for example, does not make only new soil from moment to moment but alters a new seed-moment's capacity.)

The opponent in the current passage targets the role of auxiliaries at the moment of production. Is the sprout's cause singular or multiple? If it has just one cause, then the production is not the result of some special nature induced by the various factors. Rather, the first sprout-moment must be the product of the seed-moment by itself without their influence. If, on the other hand, there are many causes active in the production of the sprout, then either the seed must be admitted to be multiple, because it is identified with the multiplicity of factors, or it is deprived of a role in the causal process, since the various factors are all different from it. Alternatively, one could hold that the various factors are all identical with the seed. In that case, all the factors would share a single identity. The auxiliary causes would be identical to the main cause—a conclusion that again would deprive them of a causal role.

Text and Translation (p. 80, lines 4–7)

> *yady ucyeta kṣityādau janayitavye tadupādānāṃ pūrvam eva kṣityādibījasya rūpāntaram iti. na tarhi bījaṃ tadanapekṣaṃ kṣityādīnāṃ janakam. tadanapekṣatve teṣām aṅkurād bhedānupapatteḥ. na cānupakārakāṇy apekṣanta iti tvayaivoktam. na ca kṣaṇasyopakārasaṃbhavo 'nyatra jananāt tasyābhedyatvād ity anekatvam api nāstīti dvitīyo 'pi vyāpakābhāvo nāsiddhaḥ.*

Objection (by objector 2 to objector 1): Given that soil, etc., are to be producers, the effect's main cause is another nature of the seed along with soil, etc., immediately prior (to the effect).

Reply (by objector 1): (Wrong.) In that case, the seed would not produce independently. It would be a producer of (a combination of) soil, etc. (which would be the producer of the sprout). If it is (nevertheless to be a producer) independent of them, then there occurs the unfortunate consequence that their sprout would be different from its sprout.

Objection (objector 2): (The seed is alone the cause.) It depends on things that are not helpers (i.e., not causes, though in some other, non-causal way required).

Reply (by objector 1): This should not be said by you. (For) there would be no possibility of assistance to the (seed) moment because they would produce something else.

Objection (by objector 2): (No, they produce the same thing) because there is no division (among them as causes collectively).

Reply (by objector 1): Then there is also not non-oneness (i.e., you are stuck with the impossibility).

Therefore, the absence of the second pair of pervaders (unity/multiplicity, one or the other of which is true of everything) is also not unestablished (in application to anything momentary).

Comments

Objector 1 now drives home the point that the seed-moment cannot produce if it is a single thing. It could be argued that "the other nature" is the single seed-moment existing along with the auxiliary causes, but that again would rob the auxiliaries of a causal role in relation to the sprout. The sprout produced will not have been produced by soil and so on as well as by the seed. If soil and so on are productive with respect to a sprout, then it must be a different sprout that they produce, not the same sprout produced by the seed.

The Buddhist also cannot argue that the auxiliary causes are depended on even though they do not assist at the moment of production, because "being dependent" just means assisting with respect to the production of just a certain effect at a certain moment. Therefore, the auxiliaries cannot rightly be called assistants if they produce something else. All this establishes that a momentary cause would be excluded from oneness if it were to be capable of producing through the assistance of auxiliary causes at the moment of production. On the other hand, the seed-moment is supposed to be a single thing. Ratnakīrti has argued that it is not split; it has a single self-nature with various non-contrary properties at any given moment. He assumes that it is a unity, one thing and not a composite, with a single nature. But the opponent appears to show that nothing momentary could be either a unity or a non-unity—a pair of pervaders, which like dependence and independence appear to apply to anything real. Thus nothing is momentary.

Text and Translation (p. 80, line 8)

tasmād asādhāraṇānaikāntikatvam gandhavattvavad iti.

(Objector 1 continues:) Therefore, (your prover) is inconclusive, because there are no similar instances, like (the alleged pervasion between earthhood and) having-smell.

Comments

Objector 1 has now concluded that a momentary thing can produce neither dependently nor independently and that it is neither one nor many. This implies, of course, that nothing momentary exists. So, if the objection is correct, then the "supporting example" in the argument, the pot, namely, would be non-momentary instead of momentary as required and thus would not be a proper example. The prover in the inference, existence, then becomes "inconclusive" in the technical sense, i.e., it is known to occur without the probandum occurring. For, that momentariness is a proper prover is not supported by any example of positive correlation between existence and momentariness. If the pot is not independently shown to be momentary, then it is among the cases at issue in the inference and cannot serve as a similar instance. In fact, all available examples are at issue, since the opponent's argument applies to everything. Nothing exists that falls outside the pair dependent-producer/independent-producer or unity/non-unity.

Thus Ratnakīrti's inference resembles the (lame!) attempt of the realist to prove that everything earthen has smell from the fact that everything earthen has earthhood. Pervasion of having-smell by being-earthen may be suggested by those things that have both. However, when the inferential subject, the *pakṣa*, is everything, it is rendered dubious by a dubious case, e.g., an earthen atom which is something not known to be smelly. Thus there is no way to overcome the doubt, just because the breadth of the *pakṣa* excludes the possibility of a similar case. Indeed, Ratnakīrti's inference is in worse straits: nothing could be a supporting example because nothing is momentary.

Text and Translation (p. 80, lines 9–14)

> *yadi manyetānupakārakā api bhavanti sahakāriṇo 'pekṣaniyāś ca kāryeṇānuvihitabhāvābhāvāc ca sahakaraṇāc ca. nanv anena krameṇākṣaṇiko 'pi bhāvo upakārakān api sahakāriṇaḥ kramavataḥ kramavatkāryeṇānukṛtānvayavyatirekān apekṣiṣyate. kariṣyate ca kramavatsahakārivaśaḥ krameṇa kāryāṇīti vyāpakānupalabdher asiddheḥ sandigdhavyatirekam anaikāntikaṃ sattvaṃ kṣaṇikatvasiddhāv iti.*

Objection (by objector 2 to objector 1:) Things that are non-assisting become also (auxiliary causes), and in that case the auxiliaries are dependent things, because certain things conform, or do not conform, to the appearance of the effect, and because there are auxiliary causes.

Reply (by objector 1:) A non-momentary thing, too, would depend upon such auxiliary causes in sequence, which in sequence are not helping, as we learn from positive and negative correlation with the effect. And so a non-momentary thing whose causal power is governed by auxiliaries produces effects in succession (depending upon the arrival of auxiliaries).

Therefore, because there is no established experience of the pervader (as pervading your alleged prover), there is doubt about the negative form (of the pervasion relationship: wherever the probandum is not, the prover is not too), and existence (your alleged prover) is inconclusive with respect to the establishment of momentariness.

Comments

The Buddhists might try to argue that the auxiliary factors have a role even though they do not assist at the moment of production because there is a correlation between the presence of the auxiliary cause at a previous moment and the production of the effect by a last seed-moment as well as a correlation between the absence of the auxiliary cause and the failure of the last seed-moment to produce. If Ratnakīrti and company try to preserve the role of the auxiliary causes in this way, however, they are admitting a kind of causal power that is not exercised immediately. The advocate of enduring things can argue that this way of conceiving auxiliary causes is applicable to the non-momentary thing. It endures and produces effects in succession due to the arrival of auxiliary factors which are not yet helping at one moment and help at another.

Objector 1, who has already shown that there are no indisputable positive correlations supporting the thesis of pervasion between existence and momentariness, now argues that there can be no negative correlations supporting the pervasion claim. A negative correlation would be between an absence of the prover and an absence of the probandum. In this case, the correlation would have to be between something known to be non-existent and also known to be non-momentary. The problem is that there can be no experience of something non-existent and so no such thing could be known. There thus remains doubt about the pervasion in its negative form just as there is doubt about the positive.

Text and Translation (p. 80, lines 15–19)

> *atra brumaḥ. kīdṛśaṃ punar apekṣārtham ādāya kṣaṇike sāpekṣānapekṣatvanivṛttir ucyate. kiṃ sahakāriṇam apekṣata iti sahakāriṇāsyopakāraḥ karttavyaḥ. atha pūrvāvasthitasyaiva bījādeḥ sahakārinā saha saṃbhūyakaraṇam. yad vā pūrvāvasthitasyety anapekṣyamilitāvasthasya karaṇamātram apekṣārthaḥ. atra prathamapakṣasyāsaṃbhāvād anapekṣaiva kṣaṇikasya, katham ubhayavyāvṛttiḥ.*

Ratnakīrti: To this we answer. When it is said that the momentary is excluded both from dependence and independence, just what type of dependence is meant? Is it dependence on auxiliary causes? Thus there would be assistance by auxiliary causes. According to this view, the seed, etc., situated in the prior moment, along with auxiliary causes would have conjunctive causal power. Or, the meaning of dependence is just the producing on the part of something situated at the prior moment when it is hooked up with independent factors. If either of these two capture the meaning (of dependence as used in your destructive dilemma), then the momentary thing is just independent. Since the momentary would be impossible on this first option (on either construal), the momentary (we affirm) is simply an independent producer. How then (given that it produces independently) is it excluded from both (dependence and independence)?

Comments

The opponent has charged that a momentary thing can produce neither dependently nor independently and that it can be neither a single thing nor a multiplicity. Ratnkīrti begins his response by distinguishing two possible ways of interpreting the first charge. If dependence means that the seed produces only in the presence of auxiliary causes, then it does produce dependently, because it has its causal power in conjunction with auxiliary factors. As he will say below, a single thing can have multiple effects. So, as an effect, the last seed-moment with its singular capacity to produce a sprout, is itself the effect of a previous seed-moment and the presence, e.g., of soil.

The problem with objector 1's conception is the supposition that it is the seed "situated in the prior moment" that comes to have conjunctive causal power. If it were recognized that the former seed-moment is distinct from the producer, the unworkable "conjunctive causal power" hypothesis could be jettisoned. If, on the other hand, it is insisted that dependence amounts to a seed existing at the previous moment with independent causal power that comes to be unleashed by meeting up with other so-styled independent factors, the opponent has a slightly different problem. The thing so situated with respect to the auxiliary factors would be an independent causal entity needing nothing from outside its group in order to produce. So you might as well admit that it is a unitary single seed-moment, or you are faced with a loss of seed identity. It is implied in both senses: the superior position is that a seed-moment is not like that; the seed-moment is an independent producer. A seed-moment so situated produces independently, since, given the auxiliaries, it is sufficient for the effect. Thus it is false that the concept of the momentary, on the Buddhist view, falls to the dilemma posed, which, in sum, Ratnakīrti reveals to be a false dilemma.

Let us add that Ratnakīrti appears to believe that a producer can be understood as producing dependently or independently depending on just what is meant by "producing." No matter how we think of it, the momentary producer is not excluded from both contraries.

Text and Translation (p. 80, lines 19–23)

yady anapekṣah kim ity upasarpaṇapratyayābhāve 'pi na karoti. karoty eva yadi syāt. svayam asaṃbhavī tu kathaṃ karotu. atha tad vā tādṛg vāsīd iti na kaścid viśeṣaḥ. tatas tādṛksvabhāvasaṃbhave 'py akaraṇaṃ sahakāriṇi nirapekṣatāṃ na kṣamata iti cet.

Objection: If it is independent, the question is why does it not produce even in the absence of the gathering conditions? If the answer is that it alone produces, how then is it to produce, it being something that by itself could not possibly produce? The objection is that there is no difference whether it was like this or like that. Therefore, even assuming the possibility that there is such a thing, its non-producing (in the absence of auxiliaries) can hardly support (the thesis of its) independence with respect to the auxiliaries.

Comments

The opponent now argues that if the seed-moment produced the sprout independently of the auxiliary conditions, it should produce even without those factors being present. If we say it can produce anyway, by its own nature even without the factors, then we again rob the auxiliaries of any role in the causal process. It would not matter whether they are present or not; the effect is produced anyway. If we admit that the last seed-moment has such a self-nature that it does not produce without the auxiliary causes, then there is no ground for saying that it produces independently.

Text and Translation (p. 80, lines 23–25)

asambaddham etat, varṇasaṃsthānasāmye 'py akartus tatsvabhāvatāyā virahāt. sa cādyātiśayajanakatvalakṣaṇaḥ svabhāvaviśeṣo na samānāsamānasantānavartiṣu bījakṣaṇeṣu sarveṣv eva saṃbhavī, kiṃ tu keṣucid eva karmakarakarapallavasahacareṣu.

Ratnakīrti: This is incoherent. Although there may be similar color and arrangement (between two distinct seed-moments), a non-producer has no self-nature of any sort. And a particular self-nature is defined by its production of the first additional capacity (within the last seed-moment). This does not hold for all seed-moments occurring in the same or in different series. Rather it holds only for some, those, namely, that are assisted by the actions of fingers and hands (etc.).

Comments

Ratnakīrti counters that the opponent's attack makes no sense because it suggests that there could be a seed-moment that is a non-producer. Production is, after all, the way a self-nature manifests itself. Everything produces an effect according to its nature. Existence is equivalent to causal capacity. Each seed-moment is a producer of either another seed-moment or of a sprout-moment. Although the last seed-moment produces independently, this independent power is provided to it by auxiliary factors acting together with its immediate seed-moment predecessor. In this way, Ratnakīrti would explain the role of auxiliary factors in the causal process. They bring about, through interaction with a previous seed-moment, a particular seed-moment that has the capacity to produce the first sprout-moment. The last seed-moment is the the first moment that has this new capacity, which it passes along to the sprout-moment that it gives rise to. Thus is inaugurated a new series. The mark of the emergence of the new series is the production of a first sprout-moment with a second moment of this new causal power that continues on in what we conveniently designate a sprout. Note that once we have a sprout, the examples become more congenial, since the sprout continues to grow, i.e., to change.

In sum, the special capacity to produce a first sprout-moment is not in all seed-moments; it is only in the ones that occur at the end of a series whose members have encountered the gathering conditions in the proper sequence. The arrival of the last required factor triggers the production of the last seed-moment which is the first to have sprout-production capacity. The first sprout-moment occurs immediately afterwards.

Text and Translation (p. 80, lines 26–28)

> *nanv ekatra kṣetre niṣpattilavanādipūrvakam ānīyaikatra kuśūle kṣiptāni sarvāṇy eva bījāni sādhāraṇarūpāṇy eva pratīyante. tat kutastyo 'yam ekabījasaṃbhavī viśeṣo yeṣām iti cet.*

Objection: The seeds that have been gathered from the same field, salted, etc., before being thrown in one and the same granary, are cognized as all alike. Thus, why is there a difference between that one seed that (according to you) can produce and the rest?

Comments

The opponent objects that it is still not clear why some seed-moments have the special potency to produce a first sprout-moment and others do not. When a crop is in the granary, the seeds are all alike. They all have the same history of being gathered from the same field and being prepared in the same way. There is thus no basis for thinking that some belong to a series where the final member produces a sprout and others do not. Insofar as the gathering conditions have not arrived, there is no way to predict which seed-series will contain the seed-moment with the special potency to produce a first sprout-moment. We are better off holding that they all have capacity to produce a sprout when they are in the granary, a capacity that endures with them though triggered only for some.

Text and Translation (p. 80, line 28–p. 81, line 4)

> *ucyate. kāraṇaṃ khalu sarvatra kārye dvividham dṛṣṭam adṛṣṭaṃ ceti sarvāstikaprasiddham etat. tataḥ pratyakṣaparokṣasahakāripratyayasākalyam asarvavidhā pratyakṣato na śakyaṃ pratipattum. tato bhaved api kāraṇasāmagrīśaktibhedāt tadṛśaḥ svabhāvabhedaḥ keṣāñcid eva bījakṣaṇānāṃ yena ta eva bījakṣaṇā ādyātiśayam aṅkuraṃ vā paramparayā janayeyuḥ. nānye ca bījakṣaṇāḥ.*

Ratnakīrti: We answer. With respect to every effect, its cause is of two kinds, known and unknown. This is commonly accepted in all the "orthodox" (i.e., non-Buddhist) schools (as well as by us). So those who do not know everything cannot know by perception an entire collection of auxiliary conditions, perceptible and imperceptible (*parokṣa*). So there can too be (contrary to your objection) such a difference in self-nature (between a seed-moment with sprout-capacity and one without), because of the difference in the power of the entire collection of causal factors, such that some seed-moments with a distinct self-nature are the only ones that produce one after the next either a first additional power or a sprout. And other seed-moments do not.

Comments

Ratnakīrti responds that we do not always know which seed-moments belong to series which will ultimately give rise to sprouts. The conditions for the production of a first sprout-moment are numerous and they are not all known, especially when the seeds are in the granary. Some will encounter the gathering conditions and lead to the production of sprouts; others will not. This is why Ratnakīrti denies the pervasion between seed-hood and capacity to produce sprouts. Not every seed-series leads to sprout-production; many continue only with further seed-production. Planting in soil, etc., changes a seed-moment without sprout-productivity into one with it. Only those seed-series that include the proper succession of gathering conditions will end with a seed-moment that has the new potency to produce a first sprout-moment. Since this is so, it is possible to distinguish a last seed-moment that has sprout-capacity from those—even those temporally very near in the series—that produce just another seed.

Text and Translation (p. 81, lines 5–6)

> *nanu yeṣūpasarpaṇapratyayasahacareṣu svakāraṇaśaktibhedād ādyātiśayajanakatvalakṣaṇo viśeṣaḥ. saṃbhāvyate sa tatrāvaśyam astīti kuto labhyam iti cet.*

Objection: With respect to whatever gathering conditions assist, a particular defined by its production of a first additional capacity, a particular (seed-moment, that is to say) that comes about because of the difference in the power of its causes, is possible (according to you), such that with respect to those conditions necessarily this (sprout-causing) seed-moment comes about. How do you know this?

Comments

The distinction between seed-moments that will eventually lead to the production of a sprout and those that will not is that the seed-moments that lead to such production belong to a series that encounters the complete set of necessary conditions, both known and unknown, that unitedly are sufficient for sprout-production. What makes such a set of conditions distinct from others is that this set actually produces a seed-moment pregnant with the capacity to produce a sprout. Immediately afterwards, a first sprout-moment is produced. The opponent asks how this view could be arrived at, implying that the difference between (a) the seed moment that does not produce a sprout but only another seed-moment and (b) that which is the first to have sprout capacity and which actually produces the sprout is not known perceptually. Ratnakīrti proceeds now to answer that the difference is known by inference.

Text and Translation (p. 81, lines 6–9)

> *aṅkurotpādād anumitād ādyātiśayalakṣaṇāt kāryād iti brumaḥ. kāraṇānupalabdhes tarhi tadabhāvaḥ eva bhaviṣyatīti cet. na. dṛśyādṛśyasamudāyasya kāraṇasyādarśane 'py abhāvāsiddheḥ kāraṇānupalabdheḥ sandigdhāsiddhatvāt.*

Ratnakīrti: We say that this is known from the effect, which is defined by the first additional capacity, as is inferred from production of the sprout. (That is to say, we know by inference from production of the sprout that there has to be a last seed-moment with the new capacity.)

Objection: Since the cause (of the sprout) is not perceived (according to you, but only inferred), only its absence, therefore, will come to be. (That is, since we would never perceive the last moment with the additional capacity that actually produces the effect, we would never expect the effect to come to be. However, we do expect it.)

Ratnakīrti: Wrong. Even though there is lacking perception of the cause, which has itself arisen from known and unknown conditions, its non-existence is not established, because non-perception of a cause does not give rise to doubt (about its existence, given that the effect from which the cause is inferred is experienced).

Comments

Ratnakīrti argues that we infer the new causal power of the last seed-moment from the sprout, the effect. That is, production of the first sprout-moment is grounds for inferring that a sufficient cause existed at the previous moment. Just because we do not perceive the last seed-moment as distinguishable from previous seed-moments by having the new capacity does not mean that this new capacity was not there. There is no cause for doubt about an effect having had a sufficient cause once the effect is produced, even though we do not know perceptually the cause's precise make-up.

Text and Translation (p. 81, lines 10–14)

> *tad ayam arthaḥ*
>
> > *pāṇisparśavataḥ kṣaṇasya na bhidā bhinnānyakālakṣaṇād*
> > *bhedo veti matadvaye mitibalaṃ yasyāstv asau jitvaraḥ.*

> *tatraikasya balaṃ nimittavirahaḥ kāryāṅgam anyasya vā*
> *sāmagrī tu na sarvathekṣaṇasahā kāryaṃ tu mānānugam. iti.*

tad evaṃ nopakāro 'pekṣārtha ity anapekṣaiva kṣaṇikasya sahakāriṣu nobhayavyāvṛttiḥ.

(Ratnakīrti continues:) Thus this is the gist.

> Either the (seed-)moment of being touched by the hand is not distinct from another moment at a distinct time,
>
> Or it is—of the two views, the one that has the force of proof will prevail.
>
> On the issue, there is the force of argument for the one option that there is no causality (on the part of the one not touched), or, for the other, that there is integration into the effect.
>
> The total causal collection (*sāmagrī*) may not in all cases support a determination (that the effect will definitely be, and so falls short of proof), but from the effect, in contrast, the thought (that the cause has occurred) has on its side right reasoning (i.e., proof).

Therefore, in this way assistance does not mean dependence. Thus the momentary, which is definitely independent, is not excluded from both (dependence and independence) with respect to auxiliaries (which do assist in the production process).

Comments

When a seed is picked up and planted in the ground, it is a different thing from its predecessor in the granary. This is proved by the occurrence of its effect, or of one its successor's effects, the sprout. The verse captures the superiority of this the Buddhist position. The action of planting the seed makes the next seed-moment different, so that its successors require one less condition to produce a sprout. The option promoted by the opponent is, in contrast, that the new seed-moment is no different than the previous one. On this view, however, being a causal factor is never sufficient for an effect. We can never tell whether at any given moment with respect to any given seed it will produce. Even though we are committed to the idea that effect and cause are necessarily connected, we cannot know whether all the other so-called causal factors are actually present. In contrast, we can be absolutely sure once we are confronted with the effect that its sufficient cause has occurred. That is why we Buddhists say that the last seed moment has a new capacity differentiating it from its predecessor seed-moment.

Now the process of change is actually gradual. The seed-moment touched by the hand may not itself produce a sprout-moment but only another seed-moment. But, we say, it has changed, such that one of its successors will have the capacity sufficient for sprout-production. In other words, a seed may well not produce a sprout as soon as it is planted in the ground. While this may be interpreted to mean that the action of the hand was irrelevant to the process, the better view is that the action of the hand has been integrated into the effect in that it has generated a seed-moment slightly closer to producing a sprout-moment than the one before it. Thus it remains possible that while the action of the hand has made a difference, a sprout-moment will not come about because some other necessary factor (such as water) never arrives. The opponent's view fails in this respect since it only collects causal factors into a set never known to be complete. The Buddhist view, in contrast, proceeds from the effect to the cause, and is able to integrate the action of the hand into the seed-series.

Thus the superiority of the Buddhist view can be seen in the fact that it is often not possible to determine which conditions are necessary for the production of an effect. But on the Buddhist picture, we reason back from the occurrence of the effect that its immediate predecessor, or predecessors, were sufficient. Thus we say that the last seed-moment has independently the capacity to produce, even though it, or its predecessors, are assisted by auxiliaries. A moment produces; that is its essential nature. What it produces may be slightly different depending on auxiliaries. But in all cases it will produce something.

Of course, auxiliaries are also causes, and with respect to a single effect auxiliaries in the causal process may need to be identified. But the point is: given the effect, we know that a sufficient cause has occurred. What we infer to be the last seed-moment is a distinct moment by virtue of having sprout-capacity. It produces independently at the moment of production, though, again, its capacity is dependent upon gathering conditions having exercised influence on its predecessors. Thus there is a role for the auxiliaries in the production process whether or not they are depended upon at the time of production.

A final note. We take it that Ratnakīrti would concede that some seed-moments have multiple causes, both a soil-moment, for example, and a seed-moment. But that does not mean that it is impossible that the last seed-moment produces independently. Indeed, qua particular *svalakṣaṇa*, the "self-characterized" produces by itself, independently.

Therefore, the opponent's charge that the momentary is excluded from both dependence and independence remains wrong, and the attack on the independence thesis is thwarted. The momentary produces independently.

Text and Translation (p. 81, lines 15–18)

> *atha saṃbhūyakaraṇam apekṣārthaḥ, tadā yadi pūrvasthitasyeti viśeṣaṇāpekṣā tadā kṣaṇikasya naivaṃ kadācid ity anapekṣaivākṣīṇā. atha pūrvasthitasyety anapekṣya militāvasthitasyaiva karaṇam apekṣārthas tadā sāpekṣataiva, nānapekṣā. tathā ca nobhayavyāvṛttir ity asiddhaḥ prathamo vyāpakānupalambhaḥ.*

(Ratnakīrti continues:) In one sense, dependence means producing conjunctively. Then, if it is held that dependence on a qualifier belongs to something situated at an earlier moment (in contrast to the independence of momentary things), then the view that the momentary is never like that (i.e., never depends on a qualifier) secures nothing but unfailing independence (for the momentary).

In another sense, dependence means producing belongs only to something properly situated with respect to auxiliaries having been encountered, irrespective of whether or not the auxiliaries exist at the moment prior (to production). In this sense, nothing but dependence (belongs to the momentary); not independence.

And in that way (too) it is not excluded from both (dependence and independence). And so non-apprehension of the first of your pairs of pervaders is unestablished (with respect to the momentary, which is definitely independent, in a certain sense, but also definitely dependent on auxiliaries, in another sense, too).

Comments

Ratnakīrti has defended the view that the momentary thing produces independently without denying that the auxiliary factors have a causal role. There is no dependence in the sense that the auxiliary factor assists a "self-characterized" particular to produce or not. Necessarily, something produces by itself. In one sense, the Buddhist denies conjunctive causal power (*saṃbhūya-karaṇa*), but he accepts dependence in another sense, looking back from an effect to find various "assistants." Relative to a delineated effect, a cause is what it is in virtue of things—seed, soil, etc.—having met up in the past. On the opponent's view, a cause is dependent in the sense that it has to join up at the moment of production with all the other factors. The difficulty seems implied that the auxiliary factors would have to act on the main cause in such a way as to create a new quality in it, the quality of conjunctivity, before it could produce. An advantage to the Buddhist account is, again, that we reason back from effects identified, accounting for changes by assistance having occurred at various points in the past. But from a metaphysical point of view, there is no time in the present for something momentary to meet up with the other factors. And so, in the metaphysical sense, Ratnakīrti insists that the momentary produces independently. The last seed-moment is sufficient for the sprout. Of course, that last seed-moment may itself have had a cause in soil as well as in its predecessor seed.

Ratnakīrti suggests that conjunctive causal power need not involve creation of a new quality, as indeed it could not in a momentary thing. Rather, conjunctive power amounts to the fact that a seed-moment gives rise to a successor with altered capacity according to the presence, or not, of assistants to the the productive act. No two seed-moments are exactly alike, even discounting time of occurrence. A momentary thing is itself simply capable of producing, but what is produced is sensitive to the assistance provided. In other words, the very fact that a moment is in conjunction with just certain other moments (the conjunction somehow internalized and contributing to what the thing is, as we infer from the effect) is sufficient for production. If this is what is meant by dependence, then it makes sense to say that the momentary produces dependently, because it does act along with auxiliaries in producing, relative to an effect delineated. In that case, we can regard the thing as dependent without violating the doctrine of momentariness. Either way, we rebut the charge that the momentary as neither dependent nor independent is not real.

Text and Translation (p. 81, lines 19–21)

> *tathaikatvānekatvayor api vyāpakayoḥ kṣaṇikād vyāvṛttir asiddhā. tattadvyāvṛttibhedam āśrityopādānatvādikālpanikasvabhāvabhede paramārthata ekenaiva svarūpeṇānekakāryaniṣpādanād ubhayavyāvṛtter abhāvāt.*

(Ratnakīrti continues:) Likewise, it has not been shown that the momentary is excluded from the pair of pervaders, oneness and non-oneness. It is not excluded from both. Utilizing (conceptually) distinct exclusions of this from that, one imagines different self-natures belong to a main cause. However, in the final analysis (or from the metaphysical point of view, *paramārthataḥ*) it is just by a single thing, with its own nature, that production takes place, production (to be sure) of multiple effects. (So, the momentary produces as one thing and not as a composite.)

Comments

Ratnakīrti makes a parallel point in rejecting the charge that the momentary can be productive neither as a single thing nor as a composite of many things working together. In the context of everyday practical activity, we use our convenient fictions to distinguish objects with which we are concerned—cows from non-cows, living from non-living things, and so on. Our conceptions overlap, and we imagine objects as having multiple natures. However, in reality, there is nothing but flux to be analyzed as series of moments in causal relationships. So, just as we conceive of independently producing particulars as producing depending on auxiliaries, so we conceive of single things grouped together and producing as composites. This is convenient, and so in a sense it is okay to say that the momentary produces as a bundle. Concept-formation, however, called *apoha* ("exclusion" of the non-F) by the Buddhists, is properly understood as grounded in sortings of particulars, which are single individuals, each unique.

In this way, we may remark, there is avoided positing universals as metaphysical entities. At the level of metaphysical reality, Ratnakīrti reminds us that it is the Buddhist position to conceive of the "self-characterized" (*svalakṣaṇa*) as free from all conceptual construction. This is an ultimate particular, singular in character, with its own unique nature. Thus the momentary is in fact one thing, and therefore not excluded from the pair oneness/multiplicity. Of course, in the way it produces as a bundle, it is said to be multiple, and again not excluded from the opponent's pair of contraries.

Here at the end Ratnakīrti states explicitly that he sees the effects of a particular moment as multiple. The conception makes room, as we have noted, for auxiliary causality, which has been at least a subtheme for quite a stretch. Soil and the like, in assisting a penultimate seed-moment become capable of sprout-production, produce new soil-moments as well as an altered seed.

Text and Translation (p. 81, lines 21–28)

> *yac ca bījasyaikenaiva svabhāvena kārakatve kṣityādīnām bījasvābhāvyāpattir*[53] *anyathā kāraṇābhede 'pi kāryabhede 'pi kāryasyāhetukatvaprasaṅgād ityuktam tad asaṅgatam. kāraṇaikatvasya kāryabhedasya ca paṭunendriyapratyakṣeṇa prasādhanāt. ekakāraṇajanyatvaikatvayor vyāpteḥ pratihatatvāt. prasaṅgasyānupadatvāt. yac ca kāraṇābhede kāryābheda ity uktaṃ tatra sāmagrīsvarūpaṃ kāraṇam abhipretam. sāmagrīsajātīyatve na kāryavijātīyatety arthaḥ. na punaḥ sāmagrīmadhyagatenaikenānekaṃ kāryaṃ na kartavyaṃ nāma, ekasmād anekotpatteḥ pratyakṣasiddhatvāt.*

Objection: The thesis that the seed is a producer through just a single self-nature has the bad consequence that soil, etc., would be implicated in the essential nature of the seed. Otherwise, the cause may be one and the same, its effects distinct (and multiple), with nevertheless the bad consequence that an effect could come to be without a cause.

Ratnakīrti: This, too, is incoherent, because a single cause with distinct (multiple) effects is proved by careful observation. That there is pervasion between oneness and being-the-product-of-a-single-cause is blocked, because a bad consequence would ensue.

Objection: The thesis that if the cause is one and the same (non-distinct, non-multiple) then the effect is one and the same (non-multiple)

---

[53] Reading *bījasvābhāvyāpatti* instead of *aṅkurasvābhāvyāpatti*.

is preserved in our idea of the cause as by nature a total collection of causal factors (*sāmagrī*). What is (really) meant here is that it is not the case that given a total collection of causal factors of a certain kind the effect will be of a different kind.

Ratnakīrti: It is, contrary to your position, not the case that a multiple effect could not be produced by one thing selected from the midst of a collection. Indeed, one thing can produce multiple effects, as is established by perception.

Comments

The opponent argued earlier that if the Buddhist imagines the seed to produce dependently through cooperation with auxiliary factors, then he faces a destructive dilemma. Either the producer is a single thing, in which case the other factors must be included in the essential nature of the seed, or the cause is a collection of many things, not a single thing with a single nature. If the auxiliaries are part of the nature of the seed, a seed defined as the producer of a sprout is not a seed unless the other factors are present. This is of course absurd. On the other hand, if the producer is a collection, the effect, too, should be a bundle. Otherwise, some of the causes will be causes without contributing to any effect. However, it is given in context that the effect is a single sprout. The opponent implies that on his view this second or right horn of the dilemma is avoided since a collection can produce a single effect. The principle of causal uniformity ("Like effects, like causes") means that a banana tree is not to be produced from a collection that includes no banana-tree seed but rather the seed of a creeper. The main point, from the opponent's perspective, is that a collection can produce a single thing. If the Buddhist insists on a single cause, he is impaled on the other horn: the single cause will do its thing, so to say, and, e.g., produce a sprout, with the other effects alleged by the Buddhist left to come about without a cause.

But Ratnakīrti embraces this the left horn, justifying his stance by reasoning parallel to the opponent's explanation why his view is not impaled on the right one. That is to say, a single cause can have multiple effects. The opponent merely presupposes that this is false. Perception, however, shows its truth. A moment of soil produces another moment of soil along with aiding a seed in its sprout-production. The opponent is right that there is no rule forbidding a mismatch between the multiplicity/unity of the cause and the multiplicity/unity of the effect. The problem with the opponent's position is the arbitrariness of the assumption that a single thing cannot have multiple effects. We have clear examples of this, i.e., shown not by dialectical argument but by perception, the bad consequence mentioned being opposition to perceptual evidence.

Text and Translation (p. 81, line 28–p. 82, line 2)

> *na caivaṃ pratyabhijñānāt kālabhede 'py abhedasiddhir ity uktaprāyam. na cendriyapratyakṣaṃ bhinnadeśaṃ sapratighaṃ dṛśyam arthadvayam ekam evopalambhayatīti kvacid upalabdham yena tatrāpi bhede śaṅkā syāt. śaṅkāyāṃ vā paṭupratyakṣasyāpy apalāpe sarvapramāṇocchedaprasaṅgād iti.*

Objection: Because of recognition (e.g, "This is that Devadatta I saw yesterday") non-difference is proved (between, e.g., Devadatta today and Devadatta yesterday), even given a difference in time.

Ratnakīrti: This, too, is not shown by your reasoning (that if the cause is one and the same, then the effect is one and the same)—which is our central point (perception of Devadatta today being different from that of him yesterday). Furthermore, it is never experienced that a known pair of objects, perceptible to the senses in distinct places and mutually opposed (e.g., sprout-producing and not-sprout-producing), causes the apprehension of just one thing, such that there too (reasonable) doubt could arise about their difference. Or, if there is doubt (about the difference or identity of something), then when sharp perception rules out one of the alternatives (as it does when we perceive some slight change with Devadatta over the course of a day), our view is established, because (otherwise) there would be the bad consequence of the destruction of all sources of knowledge (perception being accepted by all parties as the fundamental knowledge source, upon which inference, etc., depend).

Comments

Ratnakīrti continues with his strongest line of argument. Change is established perceptually. Recognition does not show identity over time, because careful observation would reveal differences. It is not possible to experience opposed or contrary properties as belonging to one and the same thing. Once we see difference and opposition, it is not possible to doubt that two objects are really identical. Or, if, fallible philosophers that we are, initially we do have doubt about something's identity or difference, it is dispelled by perception of difference entailing that there are two things. Recognition is at best sloppy perception. Careful perception would show Devadatta to be different. If such perception is not counted a prover in this instance, then perception is never a knowledge source. And if perception is not a knowledge source, all epistemology, all justification and argument through citation of *pramāṇa*, is empty talk. For, everyone admits that perception is the foundational source, without which genuine inference, testimony, or the like could not function to make us know anything. Universal skepticism would be our lot.

Text and Translation (p. 82, lines 3–5)

> *nāpi sattvahetoḥ sandigdhavyatirekatvam, kṣityāder dravyāntarasya bījasvabhāvatvenāsmābhir asvīkṛtatvāt. anupakāriṇy apekṣāyāḥ pratyākhyātatvāt vyāpakānupalambhasyāsiddhatvāyogāt.*

(Ratnakīrti continues:) Moreover, the prover, existence, does not correlate negatively (what is not momentary, that does not exist) in a way that is dubious. We do not accept that soil and the like are of the same nature as the seed, which is something else. We deny that there is any dependence that is not an assisting, because the view that experience does not establish a pervader (i.e., the probandum, here, momentariness) is wrong.

Comments

Ratnakīrti denies that he is forced to regard the other factors as part of the inherent nature of the seed. The momentary is not excluded from both dependence and independence, whether one conceives of it as producing independently after being prepared by the other conditions previously or as producing dependently in the sense of cooperation with the other factors. Having dispensed with this last objection, there remains no doubt about the negative correlations, because pervasion between momentariness and existence is established.

Text and Translation (p. 82, lines 6–11)

> *tad etau dvāv api vyāpakānupalambhāv asiddhau na kṣaṇikāt sattvaṃ nivartayata iti nāyam asādhāraṇo hetuḥ. api ca vidyamāno bhāvaḥ sādhyetarayor aniścitānvayavyatireko*

gandhavattādivad asādhāraṇo yuktaḥ. prakṛtavyāpakānupalambhāc ca sarvathārthakriyaivāsatī ubhābhyāṃ vādibhyām ubhayasmād vinivartitatvena nirāśrayatvāt. tat katham asādhāraṇānaikāntiko bhaviṣyatīty alaṃ pralāpini nirbandhena.

(Ratnakīrti continues:) Therefore, those two (alleged pairs of) pervaders also (namely, dependence/independence and oneness/non-oneness), which, not (really) being known to pervade, are not established as (genuine) pervaders (covering between them everything that is real), do not separate existence from momentariness. Therefore, our prover is not without similar examples.

Furthermore, it would be appropriate to say that an inference suffers from (the fallacy of) "no similar instance" if like the inference to having smell (from being-earthen) a presently existing thing (e.g., an earthen atom) is not shown (to possess the probandum) with certainty based on positive and negative correlations between the probandum and the prover. (But our case is not like this, since our example, a pot, has been shown both to exist and to be momentary.) And since the (alleged) pervaders under discussion do not (really) pervade, that our very (notion of existence) causal capacity is not in any way real ceases absolutely (to be of interest) for both of us disputants on both counts, since they are baseless.

Therefore, how is there to be (as you allege) inconclusiveness due to a lack of similar examples? Enough with your persistence in such chatter!

Comments

Had Ratnakīrti's example not been shown by a distinct inference to be momentary (or a pair of inferences), then it would be among the cases at issue and could not serve as a supporting example. This, as we have seen, would be like trying to prove that everything earthen has smell from the fact that anything earthen has earthhood. There a disputed case, e.g., an atom of earth, is not known to have smell through a distinct inference. But Ratnakīrti's inference is not like that. The prover, existence, is not inconclusive due to a lack of similar instances (*asādhāraṇa*). The pot is the similar instance, the example that shows the pervasion holds. Admittedly, prior to the distinct demonstration that it is momentary, it might have been controversial, like an earthen atom being smelly. But the problem is overcome by independent argument that shows it is momentary. By doing this, Ratnakīrti has met the "no-similar-instance" objection, he points out here. He has a separate way to resolve doubt about cases that are initially dubious. Thus there is no problem with the inference he has used. It has a perfectly good "similar case."

Text and Translation (p. 82, lines 12–14)

> *tad evaṃ śaktasya kṣepāyogāt samarthavyavahāragocaratvaṃ jananena vyāptam iti prasaṅgaviparyayoḥ sattvahetor api nānaikāntikatvam. ataḥ kṣaṇabhaṅgasiddhir iti sthitam.*

(Ratnakīrti continues:) Because it is impossible for a capable thing to delay, the sphere of everyday speech about capability is pervaded by producing. Therefore, our prover, existence, is also not inconclusive, given such *prasaṅga* and its transformation.

Therefore, our establishment of momentariness (*kṣaṇabhaṅga*, "destruction in a moment") stands complete.

Comments

Ratnakīrti closes by reiterating that it is his independent argumentation that is key to the success of the inference to momentariness based on positive correlations. That is, the pot, being existent, must be capable of producing an effect. If it is capable of producing a different effect in each moment, then it is a different thing at each moment. It must, however, be capable of producing a different thing at each moment, because there can be no delay in production. If the pot endured, it would have to produce the same effect over and over—which is absurd. The impossibility of delayed production is shown by the pervasion between being-spoken-of-as-a-producer and producing. Our argument from existence is therefore not inconclusive, because the pot is momentary. The proof of momentariness from existence on the basis of positive correlation is thus established, completing the first half of Ratnakīrti's *Kṣaṇabhaṅgasiddhi*.

* * * * *

iti sādharmyadṛṣṭānte 'nvayarūpavyāptyā kṣaṇabhaṅgasiddhiḥ samāptā. kṛtir iyaṃ mahāpaṇḍitaratnakīrtipādānām iti.

Thus, establishment of momentariness (*kṣaṇabhaṅgasiddhi*) by showing pervasion in a positive form where the example is a similar case has come to an end. This is the work of the revered Ratnakīrti, who is most learned.

Glossaries

Sanskrit–English

Sanskrit	English
akaraṇa	not producing
akurvan	not producing
akṣata	complete, uninjured
akṣepa	without delay, instantly
ajanaka	not producing
ajani	non-production
atikrama	going beyond, exhausting
atiśaya	additional capacity
atīta	gone by, passed, past
adhyakṣa	witness
adhyāsa	imposing
adhyavaseya	to be determined, conceptualized
adhyavasi	to determine, to conceptualize
anavadya	not unworthy to be said
anavasāra	no occasion
anavasthā	infinite regress
anavasthiti	non-presence
anivārya	unpreventable
anugama	continuity
anumāna	inference
anupakāra	not assisting
anupapatti	not possible
anupalambha	not apprehending
anupalabhdhi	misunderstanding
anubandhin	connection
anuvṛtti	consequence
anusandhāyaka	transtemporal connection

Sanskrit	**English**
anekatva	non-oneness, multiplicity
anaikāntika	inconclusive, non-uniform
aṅkura	sprout
antara	another, other
antima	final, last
antya	last in time, place, or order
anyathā	otherwise
anyonyābhava	mutual absence
anvaya	positive correlation
apara	different
aparādha	anomaly, deviation, exception
apekṣā	dependence
apramatta	careful, attentive
aprastuta	not generally accepted
abhāva	absence, non-existent
abhijñā	recognition
abhidhā	to allege, assert, or denote
abhimata	wished for, alleged, supposed
abhilāpa	everyday speech (*vyavahāra*)
abhisaṃdhā	to come to agreement
abhyupagam	to accept or assent to
ayoga	impossible, unsuitable
artha	object; meaning
arthakriyā	practical effect, causal efficiency
arthakriyākāritva	causal efficiency
arthabheda	difference of meaning
arthasāmarthya	causal efficiency
alambana	objective, independent
avagam	recognize, understand
avagāhitva	deep grasping
avadhāraṇa	understanding
avadhārya	to be known or determined

Sanskrit	English
avasthita	situated
avaśyam	necessarily, surely
avasāya	conclusion
aviṣaya	impossible, not a proper object for
aviśiṣṭa	not qualified by
aviśeṣa	no difference
avyabhicāra	non-deviation
avyāhata	not contradicted
aśakta	unable, incapable
aśakyatva	non-capacity
asaṅgata	incoherent
asaṃbhavin	impossible
asambaddham	incoherent
asahya	not capable
asādhāraṇa	without similar cases
asthairya	instability, unsteadiness
ākṣipta	implied
ākṣepa	dependent on
āgantuka	acquired
ācakṣ	to state
ābhāsa	appearance
āyāta	arrived at
āropa	assuming the form, imposition, projection
āvah	to lead to
āsajyate	to be attatched
āśraya	base, support, locus
ucita	appropriate
upātta	accepted
utpāda	production
utsārīta	established
udāsīna	inactive
uccheda	cutting off

Sanskrit	English
upapatti	possible
upanyasitum	to understand, to infer
upanyāsa	adducing
upapanna	appropriate
upalambha	apprehending
upalambhaka	perception, apprehenion
upalabdha	understood, apprehended, experienced
upalabhyamāna	experiencing, apprehending
upasaṃhartum	to assert together
upasaṃhāravat	conclusive
upasarpanapratayaya	gathering conditions
upasthā	to remember (causative: to establish)
upādāna	main cause; receiver, apprehender
upādeya	accessible, apprehended
ekatara	one of two, either one or the other
ekatra	in one place
ekatva	oneness, unity
ekāntika	non-deviating
aupacārika	metaphorical, derivative
karaṇa	producing, causing, making
karaṇatva	causality
karoti	produces
karttavya	to be determined
kartṛ	doer, subject of a sentence
kāraka	doing
kāraṇa	cause
kāraṇatva	causality
kāraṇa-buddhi	awareness of the cause
kārin	doing, producing
kārya	effect, thing to be produced
kāryāṅga	integration into the effect
kārya-karaṇa	producing the effect

Sanskrit	English
kārya-karaṇa-bhāva	causality
kārya-buddhi	awareness of the effect
kāryatva	effecthood
kāla	time
kurvāṇa	doing, making
kuśūla	granary
krama	sequence
kramika	successive
kriyā	action, capacity
kṣati	defect, fault, destruction
kṣaṇa	moment
kṣaṇabhaṅgasiddhi	proof of destruction in a moment
kṣaṇabhāvin	existing moment
kṣaṇika	momentary
gṛhīta	grasped, cognized
gocara	scope, range
grahaṇa	grasping
grāmya	vulgar, indecent, low
grāhaka	grasping
ghaṭa	pot
jagat	moving
janakatva	causation, production
janana	producing
jāta	born, produced
jñāpaka	making known
jñāna	cognition
tathātva	condition of being thus
tadānīm	at that time
tarala	transitory
tirobhāva	concealing, dark
darśana	philosophical system; seeing
durvāra	unavoidable, irresistible

Sanskrit	**English**
dūra	firmly
dṛṣṭa	seen
dṛṣṭānta	example
dharma	quality, property
dharmin	possessing properties
dhrauvya	stability
nikṣipta	thrown out
nija	innate
nidarśana	example
nimitta	cause, instrument
niyata	restriction, rule-bound
niyama	rule, law
nirarthanka	meaningless
nirastatva	rejection
nirākaraṇa	refutation
nirīha	motionless
niruddha	blocked, rejected, held back
nirūpaṇa	determining
nirūpyamāna	being determined
nirdalana	splitting up
nirmūlita	unsupported
nivṛitti	cessation, disappearance
niścaya	certainty
niścetavya	to be cognized with certainty
niṣedha	denial
niṣṭaṅkita	expressed
niṣpanna	produced
nyāya	argument
pakṣa	inferential subject, case at issue
pakṣīkṛta	taken as the inferential subject
padārtha	object, category
paraspara	mutual

Sanskrit	English
parābhyupagama	refutation
parāvṛtta	excluded
parāvṛtti	exclusion
parikalpa	imagination, illusion
parigal	to vanish
parijñāna	specific cognition
paribhāṣā	technical rule
parokṣa	imperceptible
parokṣārtha	absent or invisible object
parihāra	exclusion
paryante	in the end
paryāya	synonym
pātra	capable person
pāramārthika	literal, relating to ultimate truth
pṛthak	different from, seperate from
prakāra	way of appearing
pratikṣaṇam	at every moment, continually
pratiniyata	rule-bound
pratipatti	understanding
pratipādaka	establishing
pratibaddha	opposed
pratiyogin	absentee
pratihata	obstructed, impeded
pratīta	recognized, known
pratīti	following from
pratisandhātṛ	one who recollects
pratyakṣa	perception
pratyanīka	contrary
pratyabhijñāna	recognition
pradīpa	lamp
prapañcatā	demonstration
prabheda	division, kind

Sanskrit	**English**
pramāṇa	source of knowledge
prayāsa	exertion, effort
prayukta	use, employment
prayoga	formal reconstruction
pralāpa	chatter
pravṛtta	existing
pravṛtti	activity, employment, usage, mention
prasaṅga	unfortunate consequence, reductio argument
prasaṅgaviparyaya	inferential tranformation of a *prasaṅga*
prasara	consequence
prasādhaka	establish
prasādhana	proof
prasiddham	established
prastuta	in focus
prādhānya	superior power
bādhaka	opposing, defeating, ruling out
bādhana	blocking, defeating
bīja	seed
buddhi	apprehension
bhājana	belonging to
bhāvitva	existence
bhāvin	existing, possessing existence
bhinna	different, distinct, split, divided
bhīru	afraid, timid
bhūta	being, existent
bheda	difference, distinction
milita	united, joined
yogitva	being suitable
yogya	suitable
yukta	appropriate
lakṣaṇa	definition, mark, characteristic

Sanskrit	English
lūna	cut off
varāka	wretched, low
vartamāna	existing in the present
vastu	thing, object, real, each and everāy thing
vastutva	being a real thing
vāsanā	memory impression
vikalpa	construct, notion, imagination, option
vikalparūḍha	mounted on options (eliminative argument)
vidha	kind, type
vidhāna	assertion
vidhibhūta	established by rule
vidhvaṃsa	destruction
vipakṣa	dissimilar case
viparyaya	transformation
vipratipanna	contrary to what is understood
vimarśa	appreciation, consideration
virodha	contrariety, opposition, contradiction
virūddha	contrary, opposed
vilamba	hesitation
vilasita	manifest
viśiṣṭa	qualified by
viśeṣa	different, particular
viśeṣaṇa	qualifier
viśeṣya	to be qualified
viṣaya	scope, sphere, range; object
vaiyarthya	uselessness
vyaktavya	to be spoken of
vyatireka	negative correlation
vyapadeśa	speech
vyabhicāra	non-deviating
vyaya	destruction
vyavaccheda	specification

Sanskrit	**English**
vyavahāra	what is said, everyday speech and behavior
vyāpaka	pervader
vyāpta	pervaded
vyāpti	pervasion
vyāvṛtti	exclusion
vyāvṛttibheda	difference in what is excluded
śakta	able, capable
śaktatva	capability, capacity
śakti	power, capacity
śaktīsvīkāra	link of words and objects, conventional meaning
śakyatva	capacity
śaṅkā	doubt
śabda	word, testimony
samāropaka	superimposing
saṃbhandha	connection
saṃbhava	possibility
saṃbhāvanā	supposition
saṃbhūyakaraṇa	conjunctive production
saṃgam	to be correct, go together
saṃsarga	relation
sakala	entire, complete
sat	existent entity
sattā	existence
sattvalakṣaṇa	definition of existence, mark of existence
sattvahetu	an inference whose prover is existence
sadṛṣa	similar
santāna	series
sandigdha	doubtful
sandeha	doubt
sapakṣa	similar case
samartha	capable, able

Sanskrit	English
samarthakṣaṇa	capable moment
samavāya	inherence
samīha	striving after
samvittī	collective self-cognition
samśaya	doubt
sahakārin	auxiliary cause
sahakārī-sākalyam	auxiliary factor
sākṣāt	immediately
sādhaka	showing, convincing
sādhana	prover (*hetu*)
sādhāraṇa	common
sādharmya	similarity of property
sādhya	that which is to be proved, probandum
sāmagrī	complete collection of causal factors
sāmānya	universal
sthita	occuring, arising
sthira	enduring
svākāra	own form
svakārya	own effect
svabhāva	self-nature
svabhāvahetu	inference from a thing's self-nature
svatantra	independent, self-dependent
svarūpa	own nature, own form
svalakṣaṇa	self-characterized particular
svasaṃvedana	cognition as self-conscious, self-illumining
svīkṛ	to make one's own, to accept
hetu	prover; cause
hetucakra	wheel of causes
hetvābhāsa	pseudo-prover

English–Sanskrit

English	Sanskrit
able, capable	śakta
absence, non-existent	abhāva
absent or invisible object	parokṣārtha
absentee	pratiyogin
accepted	upātta
accessible, apprehended	upādeya
acquired	āgantuka
action, capacity	kriyā
activity, employment, usage, mention	pravṛtti
additional capacity	atiśaya
adducing	upanyāsa
afraid, timid	bhīru
anomaly, deviation, exception	aparādha
another, other	antara
appearance	ābhāsa
appreciation, consideration	vimarśa
apprehending	upalambha
apprehension	buddhi
appropriate	ucita, upapanna, yukta
argument	nyāya
arrived at	āyāta
assertion	vidhāna
assuming the form, imposition, projection	āropa
at every moment, continually	pratikṣaṇam
at that time	tadānīm
auxiliary cause	sahakārin
auxiliary factor	sahakārī-sākalyam
awareness of the cause	kāraṇa-buddhi
awareness of the effect	kārya-buddhi
base, support, locus	āśraya

English	Sanskrit
being a real thing	vastutva
being determined	nirūpyamāna
being suitable	yogitva
being, existent	bhūta
belonging to	bhājana
blocked, rejected, held back	niruddha
blocking, defeating	bādhana
born, produced	jāta
capability, capacity	śaktatva
capable moment	samarthakṣaṇa
capable person	pātra
capable, able	samartha
capacity	śakyatva
careful, attentive	apramatta
causal efficiency	arthakriyākāritva, arthasāmarthya
causality	karaṇatva, kāraṇatva, kārya-karaṇa-bhāva
causation, production	janakatva
cause	kāraṇa
cause, instrument	nimitta
certainty	niścaya
cessation, disappearance	nivṛitti
chatter	pralāpa
cognition	jñāna
cognition as self-conscious, self-illumining	svasaṃvedana
collective self-cognition	samvittī
common	sādhāraṇa
complete collection of causal factors	sāmagrī
complete, uninjured	akṣata
concealing, dark	tirobhāva
conclusion	avasāya

English	Sanskrit
conclusive	upasaṃhāravat
condition of being thus	tathātva
conjunctive production	saṃbhūyakaraṇa
connection	anubandhin, saṃbhandha
consequence	anuvṛtti, prasara
construct, notion, imagination, option	vikalpa
continuity	anugama
contrariety, opposition, contradiction	virodha
contrary	pratyanīka
contrary to what is understood	vipratipanna
contrary, opposed	virūddha
cut off	lūna
cutting off	uccheda
deep grasping	avagāhitva
defect, fault, destruction	kṣati
definition of existence, mark of existence	sattvalakṣaṇa
definition, mark, characteristic	lakṣaṇa
demonstration	prapañcatā
denial	niṣedha
dependence	apekṣā
dependent on	ākṣepa
destruction	vidhvaṃsa, vyaya
determining	nirūpaṇa
difference in what is excluded	vyāvṛttibheda
difference of meaning	arthabheda
difference, distinction	bheda
different	apara
different from, seperate from	pṛthak
different, distinct, split, divided	bhinna
different, particular	viśeṣa
dissimilar case	vipakṣa
division, kind	prabheda

English	Sanskrit
doer, subject of a sentence	kartṛ
doing	kāraka
doing, making	kurvāṇa
doing, producing	kārin
doubt	śaṅkā, sandeha, samśaya
doubtful	sandigdha
effect, thing to be produced	kārya
effecthood	kāryatva
enduring	sthira
entire, complete	sakala
establish	prasādhaka
established	utsārīta, prasiddham
established by rule	vidhibhūta
establishing	pratipādaka
everyday speech (*vyavahāra*)	abhilāpa
example	dṛṣṭānta, nidarśana
excluded	parāvṛtta
exclusion	parāvṛtti, parihāra, vyāvṛtti
exertion, effort	prayāsa
existence	bhāvitva, sattā
existent entity	sat
existing	pravṛtta
existing in the present	vartamāna
existing moment	kṣaṇabhāvin
existing, possessing existence	bhāvin
experiencing, apprehending	upalabhyamāna
expressed	niṣṭaṅkita
final, last	antima
firmly	dūra
following from	pratīti
formal reconstruction	prayoga
gathering conditions	upasarpanapratayaya

English	**Sanskrit**
going beyond, exhausting	atikrama
gone by, passed, past	atīta
granary	kuśūla
grasped, cognized	gṛhīta
grasping	grahaṇa, grāhaka
hesitation	vilamba
imagination, illusion	parikalpa
immediately	sākṣāt
imperceptible	parokṣa
implied	ākṣipta
imposing	adhyāsa
impossible	asaṃbhavin
impossible, not a proper object for	aviṣaya
impossible, unsuitable	ayoga
in focus	prastuta
in one place	ekatra
in the end	paryante
inactive	udāsīna
incoherent	asaṅgata, asambaddham
inconclusive, non-uniform	anaikāntika
independent, self-dependent	svatantra
inference	anumāna
inference from a thing's self-nature	svabhāvahetu
inference whose prover is existence	sattvahetu
inferential subject, case at issue	pakṣa
inferential tranformation of a *prasaṅga*	prasaṅgaviparyaya
infinite regress	anavasthā
inherence	samavāya
innate	nija
instability, unsteadiness	asthairya
integration into the effect	kāryāṅga
kind, type	vidha

English	**Sanskrit**
lamp	pradīpa
last in time, place, or order	antya
link of words and objects, conventional meaning	śaktīsvīkāra
literal, relating to ultimate truth	pāramārthika
main cause; receiver, apprehender	upādāna
making known	jñāpaka
manifest	vilasita
meaningless	nirarthanka
memory impression	vāsanā
metaphorical, derivative	aupacārika
misunderstanding	anupalabhdhi
moment	kṣaṇa
momentary	kṣaṇika
motionless	nirīha
mounted on options (eliminative argument)	vikalparūḍha
moving	jagat
mutual	paraspara
mutual absence	anyonyābhava
necessarily, surely	avaśyam
negative correlation	vyatireka
no difference	aviśeṣa
no occasion	anavasāra
non-capacity	aśakyatva
non-deviating	ekāntika, vyabhicāra
non-deviation	avyabhicāra
non-oneness, multiplicity	anekatva
non-presence	anavasthiti
non-production	ajani
not apprehending	anupalambha
not assisting	anupakāra
not capable	asahya

English	Sanskrit
not contradicted	avyāhata
not generally accepted	aprastuta
not possible	anupapatti
not producing	akaraṇa, akurvan, ajanaka
not qualified by	aviśiṣṭa
not unworthy to be said	anavadya
object, category	padārtha
object; meaning	artha
objective, independent	alambana
obstructed, impeded	pratihata
occuring, arising	sthita
one of two, either one or the other	ekatara
one who recollects	pratisandhātṛ
oneness, unity	ekatva
opposed	pratibaddha
opposing, defeating, ruling out	bādhaka
otherwise	anyathā
own effect	svakārya
own form	svākāra
own nature, own form	svarūpa
perception	pratyakṣa
perception, apprehenion	upalambhaka
pervaded	vyāpta
pervader	vyāpaka
pervasion	vyāpti
philosophical system; seeing	darśana
positive correlation	anvaya
possessing properties	dharmin
possibility	saṃbhava
possible	upapatti
pot	ghaṭa
power, capacity	śakti

English	Sanskrit
practical effect, causal efficiency	arthakriyā
produced	niṣpanna
produces	karoti
producing	janana
producing the effect	kārya-karaṇa
producing, causing, making	karaṇa
production	utpāda
proof	prasādhana
proof of destruction in a moment	kṣaṇabhaṅgasiddhi
prover (*hetu*)	sādhana
prover; cause	hetu
pseudo-prover	hetvābhāsa
qualified by	viśiṣṭa
qualifier	viśeṣaṇa
quality, property	dharma
recognition	abhijñā, pratyabhijñāna
recognize, understand	avagam
recognized, known	pratīta
refutation	nirākaraṇa, parābhyupagama
rejection	nirastatva
relation	saṃsarga
restriction, rule-bound	niyata
rule-bound	pratiniyata
rule, law	niyama
scope, range	gocara
scope, sphere, range; object	viṣaya
seed	bīja
seen	dṛṣṭa
self-characterized particular	svalakṣaṇa
self-nature	svabhāva
sequence	krama

English	Sanskrit
series	santāna
showing, convincing	sādhaka
similar	sadṛṣa
similar case	sapakṣa
similarity of property	sādharmya
situated	avasthita
source of knowledge	pramāṇa
specific cognition	parijñāna
specification	vyavaccheda
speech	vyapadeśa
splitting up	nirdalana
sprout	aṅkura
stability	dhrauvya
striving after	samīha
successive	kramika
suitable	yogya
superimposing	samāropaka
superior power	prādhānya
supposition	saṃbhāvanā
synonym	paryāya
taken as the inferential subject	pakṣīkṛta
technical rule	paribhāṣā
that which is to be proved, probandum	sādhya
thing, object, real, each and every thing	vastu
thrown out	nikṣipta
time	kāla
to accept or assent to	abhyupagam
to allege, assert, or denote	abhidhā
to assert together	upasaṃhartum
to be attatched	āsajyate
to be cognized with certainty	niścetavya
to be correct, go together	saṃgam

English	**Sanskrit**
to be determined	karttavya
to be determined, conceptualized	adhyavaseya
to be known or determined	avadhārya
to be qualified	viśeṣya
to be spoken of	vyaktavya
to come to agreement	abhisaṃdhā
to determine, to conceptualize	adhyavasi
to lead to	āvah
to make one's own, to accept	svīkṛ
to remember (causative: to establish)	upasthā
to state	ācakṣ
to understand, to infer	upanyasitum
to vanish	pạrigal
transformation	viparyaya
transitory	tarala
transtemporal connection	anusandhāyaka
unable, incapable	aśakta
unavoidable, irresistible	durvāra
understanding	avadhāraṇa, pratipatti
understood, apprehended, experienced	upalabdha
unfortunate consequence, reductio argument	prasaṅga
united, joined	milita
universal	sāmānya
unpreventable	anivārya
unsupported	nirmūlita
use, employment	prayukta
uselessness	vaiyarthya
vulgar, indecent, low	grāmya
way of appearing	prakāra
what is said, everyday speech and behavior	vyavahāra
wheel of causes	hetucakra

English	**Sanskrit**
wished for, alleged, supposed	abhimata
without delay, instantly	akṣepa
without similar cases	asādhāraṇa
witness	adhyakṣa
word, testimony	śabda
wretched, low	varāka

Bibliography

Bagchi, Sitansusekhar. 1953. *Inductive Reasoning*. Calcutta: Munishchandra Sinha.

Bagchi, S., ed. 1970. *Mahāyānasūtrālaṅkāra of Asaṅga*. Darbhanga: Mithila Institute.

Bhaduri, Sadananda. 1975. *Studies in Nyāya-Vaiśeṣika Metaphysics*. Poona: Bhandarkar Oriental Research Institute.

Bhatt, S.R. and Anu Mehrotra. 2000. *Buddhist Epistemology*. London: Greenwood Press.

Chakrabarti, Arindam. 1992. "I Touch What I Saw." *Philosophy and Phenomenological Research* 52.

Chakrabarti, Kisor. 1987. "The Svabhāvahetu in Dharmakīrti's Logic." *Philosophy East and West* 37.

———. 1999. *Classical Indian Philosophy of Mind*. Albany: SUNY.

Chatterjee, S.C. 1939. *The Nyāya Theory of Knowledge: A Critical Study of Some Problems in Logic and Metaphysics*. Calcutta: Calcutta University Press.

Chaudhary, Radhakrisna. 1975. *The University of Vikramaśīla*. Patna: The Bihar Research Society.

Dravid, N.S., trans. 1995. *Ātmatattvaviveka by Udayanacarya*. Shimla: Indian Institute of Advanced Study.

Dvivedin, M.V. and Dravida, L.S., eds. 1986. *Ātmatattvaviveka*. Calcutta: The Asiatic Society.

Ganeri, Jonardon. 2000. "Cross-Modality and the Self." *Philosophy and Phenomenological Research*, Vol. 61, No. 3 (Nov. 2000), pp. 639–657.

Gangopadhyaya, Mrinalkanti, trans. 1982. *Gautama's Nyāyasūtra with Vātsyāyana's Commentary*. Calcutta: Indian Studies.

Gokhale, Pradeep, trans. 1997. *Hetubindu of Dharmakīrti (A Point on Probans)*. Delhi: Sri Satguru Publications.

Goyal, S.R. 1987. *A History of Indian Buddhism*. Meerut: Kusumanjali Prakashan.

Gupta, Rita. 1990. *Essays on Dependent Origination and Momentariness*. Calcutta: Sanskrit Pustak Bhandar.

Hattori, Masaaki, trans. 1968. *Dignāga on Perception*. Cambridge: Harvard University Press.

Hayes, Richard. 1988. *Dignāga on the Interpretation of Signs*. Dordrecht: Kluwer Academic Publishers.

Jha, Ganganatha, trans. 1919. *The Nyāyasūtras of Gautama with the Bhāṣya of Vātsyāyana and the Vārttika of Uddyotakara*. Vols. 1–4. Delhi: Motilal Banarsidass.

———. 1939. *The Tattvasaṅgraha of Śāntarakṣita with the Commentary of Kamalaśīla*. Vols. 1 & 2. Baroda: Oriental Institute.

Jhalakikar, Bhimacarya, compiler. 1978. *Nyāyakośa* (*Dictionary of Technical Terms of Indian Philosophy*). Ed. and rev. Vasudev Shastri Abhyankar. Poona: Bhandarkar Oriental Research Institute.

Kajiyama, Yuichi. 1998. *An Introduction to Buddhist Philosophy: An Annotated Translation of the Tarkabhāṣā of Mokṣākaragupta* Wien: Arbeitskreis fur Tibetische und Buddhistische Studien Universitat Wien.

Keay, John. 2000. *India: A History*. New York: Atlantic Monthly Press.

Kher, Chitrarekha and Kumar, Shiv, trans. 1987. *Ātmatattvaviveka of Udayana*. Delhi: Eastern Book Linkers.

Krishnamacharya, Embar, ed. 1984. *Tattvasaṅgraha of Śāntarakṣita with the Commentary of Kamalaśīla*. Vol. 1. Baroda: Oriental Institute.

———. 1988. *Tattvasaṅgraha of Śāntarakṣita with the Commentary of Kamalaśīla*. Vol. 2. Baroda: Oriental Institute.

Laine, Joy. 1998. "Udayana's Refutation of the Buddhist Thesis of Momentariness in the Ātmatattvaviveka." *Journal of Indian Philosophy 26*.

Lamotte, Etienne. 1988. *History of Indian Buddhism from the Origins to the Śāka Era*. Translated from the French by Sara Webb-Boin. Louvain-La-Neuve: Insitut Orientaliste.

Maitra, Susil Kumar. 1974. *Fundamental Questions of Indian Metaphysics and Logic*. Calcutta: University of Calcutta Press.

Matilal, Bimal. 1986. *Perception: An Essay on Classical Indian Theories of Knowledge*. Oxford: Clarendon Press.

———. 1989. "Nyāya Critique of the Buddhist Doctrine of No-Soul." *Journal of Indian Philosophy* 17.

———. 1998. *The Character of Logic in India*. Edited by Jonardon Ganeri and Heeraman Tiwari. Albany: SUNY.

McDermott, A.C. Senape, trans. 1969. *Ratnakīrti's Kṣaṇabhaṅgasiddhiḥ Vyatirekātmikā: An Eleventh-Century Buddhist Logic of 'Exists.'* Dordrecht: D. Reidel.

———. 1972. "Mr. Ruegg on Ratnakīrti." *Journal of Indian Philosophy* 2, pp. 16–20.

Mimaki, Katsumi. 1976. *La Réfutation Bouddhique de la Permanence des Choses (Sthirasiddhidūṣana) et la Preuve de la Momentanéité des Choses (Kṣaṇabhaṅgasiddhi)*. Paris: Institute de Civilisation Indienne.

Mohanty, J.N. 2000. *Classical Indian Philosophy.* Lanham: Rowan and Littlefield.

Mookerji, Satkari. 1975. *The Buddhist Philosophy of Universal Flux: An Exposition of the Philosophy of Critical Realism as Expounded by the School of Dignāga*. Delhi: Motilal Banarsidass.

Mookerji, Satkari and Nagasaki, H., trans. 1964. *The Pramāṇavārttika of Dharmakīrti*. Nava Nalanda Mahavihara.

Phillips, Stephen H. 1995. *Classical Indian Metaphysics: Refutations of Realism and the Emergence of "New Logic."* Chicago: Open Court.

Phillips, Stephen H. and N.S. Ramanuja Tatacharya. 2002. *Gaṅgeśa on the Upādhi, the "Inferential Undercutting Condition": Introduction, Translation and Explanation*. New Delhi: Indian Council of Philosophical Research.

Potter, Karl H. 1983. *Encyclopedia of Indian Philosophy*. Vol. 1. Delhi: Motilal Banarsidass.

Pradhan, P., ed. 1975. *Abhidharmakośabhāṣya of Vasubandhu*. Revised Second Edition. Patna: K.P. Jayaswal Research Intitute.

Pruden, Leo, trans. 1988. *Abhidharmakośabhāṣya, from the French translation by Poussin*. Berkeley: Asian Humanities Press.

Ramaiah, C. 1978. *The Problem of Change and Identity in Indian Philosophy*. Tirupati: Sri Venkateswara University.

Rospatt, Alexander. 1995. *The Buddhist Doctrine of Momentariness*. Stuttgart: Franz Steiner Verlag.

Routley, R. 1966a. "On Significance Theory." *Australasian Journal of Philosophy* 44 (1966), pp. 172–209

———. 1966b. "Some Things Do Not Exist." *Notre Dame Journal of Formal Logic* 7 (July 1966), pp. 251–76.

Ruegg, D. Seyfort. 1970. "On Ratnakīrti." *Journal of Indian Philosophy* 1, pp. 300–309.

Sanghavi, Sukhalji and Jinavijayaji, Muni Shri., eds. 1949. *Hetubindu-ṭīkā*. Baroda: Oriental Institute.

Sastri, Dhunghiraja, ed. 1997. *Ātmatattvaviveka of Sri Udayanācarya*. Varanasi: Chowkhamba Sanskrit Series Office.

Śāstrī, Haraprāsada, ed. 1910. *Six Buddhist Nyāya Tracts*. Calcutta: The Asiatic Society of Bengal.

Schweizer, Paul. 1994. "Momentary Consciousness and Buddhist Epistemology." *Journal of Indian Philosophy* 22.

Shastri, Swami Dwarikadas, ed. 1968. *Pramāṇavārttika of Ācarya Dharmakīrti*. Varanasi: Bhauddha Bharati.

Shastri, D. N. 1964. *Critique of Indian Realism: A Study of the Conflict Between the Nyāya-Vaiśeṣika and Buddhist Dignāga School*. Agra University and Motilal Banarsidass.

Shukla, Karunesha, ed. 1973. *Śrāvakabhūmi of Acarya Asaṅga*. Patna: K.P. Jayaswal Research Institute.

Singh, Amar. 1984. *The Heart of Buddhist Philosophy: Dignāga and Dharmakīrti*. New Delhi: Munshiram Manoharlal.

———. 1995. *The Sautrāntika Analytical Philosophy*. Delhi: Dharma Cakra Publications.

Staal, J.F. 1973. "The Concept of Pakṣa in Indian Logic." *Journal of Indian Philosophy* 2, no. 2.

———. 1962. "Negation and the Law of Contradiction in Indian Thought." *Bulletin of the School of Oriental and African Studies* 25.

Stcherbatsky, Th. 1930. *Buddhist Logic*. Vols. 1 and 2. Delhi: Motilal Banarsidass.

Steinkellner, Ernst, ed. 1991. *Studies in the Buddhist Epistemological Tradition: Proceedings of the Second International Dharmakīrti Conference*. Wien: Osterreichische Akademie der Wissenschaften.

Tachikawa, Musashi. 1981. *The Structure of the World in Udayana's Realism*. Dordrecht: D. Reidel.

Tarkatirtha, Amerendramohan. 1985. *Nyāyadarṣanam* (*Nyāyasūtra* with four commentaries), the *Nyāyasūtra-bhāṣya* of Vātsyāyana, the *Nyāyasūtra-vārttika* of Uddyotakara, the *Nyāyasūtravārttika-tātpāryaṭīkā* of Vācaspati Miśra, and the *Vṛtti* of Viśvanātha. Taranatha Nyayatarkatirtha and H.K. Tarkatirtha, co-editors. Calcutta Sanskrit Series 18. 1936–1944. Reprint, New Delhi, Munshiram Manoharlal.

Tatia, Nathmal, ed. 1976. *Abhidharmasamuccayabhāṣya*. Patna: K.P. Jayaswal Research Institute.

Thakur, Anantalal. 1975. *Ratnakīrtibandhāvali*. Patna: Kashi Prasad Jayaswal Research Institute.

———. 1987. *Jñānasrīmitrabandhāvali*. Patna: Kashi Prasad Jayaswal Research Institute.

Tripathi, Chhotelal. 1970. "The Problem of Svalakṣaṇas in the Sautrāntika Epistemology." *Journal of the Oriental Institute* 20.

Vidyabhusana, Satis Chandra. 1971. *A History of Indian Logic*. Delhi: Motilal Banarsidass.

Vyas, C.S. 1991. *Buddhist Theory of Perception*. New Delhi: Navrang.

Warren, Henry Clarke. 1963. *Buddhism in Translation*. New York: Athenum.

Woo, Jeson. 1999. The "Kṣaṇabhaṅgasiddhi-Anvayātmikā": An Eleventh-Century Buddhist Work on Existence and Causal Theory. University of Pennsylvania Dissertation. UMI microform #9926216.

Index

G

I

J

K

M

N

O

P

T

U

V

W

Y